本成果受到中国人民大学"中央高校建设世界一流大学（学科）和特色发展引导专项资金"支持，项目批准号：15XNLG09

大国学研究文库

伊犁河流域额鲁特人
托忒文文献荟萃

The Collection of Clear Script Document of the Ölets in the Ili River Basin （First Collection） Vol I

（第一辑） 第一卷

叶尔达◎主编

中国社会科学出版社

图书在版编目（CIP）数据

伊犁河流域额鲁特人托忒文文献荟萃. 第一辑：全三卷：蒙古语／
叶尔达主编 . 一北京：中国社会科学出版社，2016.10
（大国学研究文库）
ISBN 978 - 7 - 5161 - 8496 - 7

Ⅰ.①伊… Ⅱ.①叶… Ⅲ.①厄鲁特—古籍—汇编—中国—蒙古语
（中国少数民族语言） Ⅳ.①K289

中国版本图书馆 CIP 数据核字（2016）第 156686 号

出 版 人 赵剑英
责任编辑 史慕鸿
责任校对 李四新
责任印制 戴 宽

出 版 中国社会科学出版社
社 址 北京鼓楼西大街甲 158 号
邮 编 100720
网 址 http://www.csspw.cn
发 行 部 010 - 84083685
门 市 部 010 - 84029450
经 销 新华书店及其他书店

印刷装订 北京君升印刷有限公司
版 次 2016 年 10 月第 1 版
印 次 2016 年 10 月第 1 次印刷

开 本 710×1000 1/16
印 张 58.25
字 数 508 千字
定 价 298.00 元（全三卷）

凡购买中国社会科学出版社图书，如有质量问题请与本社营销中心联系调换
电话:010 - 84083683

信仰与地域文字遗产
（代　序）

叶尔达

　　伊犁河主要源头之一的特克斯河，发源于海拔 6995 米高处的天山山脉第二高峰汗腾格里北侧，向东流经中国新疆维吾尔自治区伊犁哈萨克自治州昭苏盆地和特克斯谷地，又转向北穿越伊什格力克山，与右岸支流巩乃斯河汇合后成为伊犁河。伊犁河西流，在霍尔果斯一带进入哈萨克斯坦境内，流经诸多峡谷、沙漠地区，注入巴尔喀什湖。

　　自 2000 年至 2015 年的 15 年间，笔者在新疆伊犁河流域进行了无间断的长期田野调查。以搜集托忒文文献为主要目的，其调查对象主要是在天山山脉北麓伊犁河上游的额鲁特蒙古民间。

　　额鲁特人是四卫拉特的重要组成部分。现在生活在新疆伊犁河流域的额鲁特人，大部分是在 1755—1757 年被清朝征服后余生的准噶尔部幸存者后裔。其中一部分人则是 1771 年从伏尔加河流域东归的咱雅班第达那木海扎木苏沙比纳尔之后裔。

　　在 1648 年，和硕特部（四卫拉特部落之一）著名高僧咱雅班第达创制了托忒文，迄今已有 360 多年的历史。在蒙古族文字史上，使用时间最长的是回鹘式蒙古文，其次就是托忒文了。无论是被使用的时间之长，还是所遗留下来的文献之多，托忒文仅次于回鹘蒙古文。可想而知，在蒙古族文化史上，托忒文文献具有不可忽视的重要地位。

　　然而，随着历史的车轮进入 20 世纪，托忒文却逐渐被人们所遗弃。最初 20 世纪 20 年代，俄罗斯境内的卡尔梅克人，之后在 20 世纪 40 年代，蒙古国西部的卫拉特人，分别开始使用基里尔文。自 20 世纪 70 年代开始，中国新疆的卫拉特人也对自己所使用的文字进行了改革。到了 90

年代，新疆境内的蒙古人均开始使用回鹘式蒙古文（卫拉特人称为胡都木蒙古文），于是托忒文完全被淘汰。在蒙古文化史上，从时间上来看，托忒文虽然使用到现代，却成为被我们所遗弃的蒙古文字之一。

目前，中国、俄罗斯和蒙古国是收藏托忒文文献最多的三个国家。据笔者通过田野调查所获取的资料来判断，新疆伊犁河流域是国际上收藏托忒文文献最多，并且是保存量最丰富的地域。他们收藏着上千部托忒文珍贵古籍，但遗憾的是，我们还没有完全开发利用该地区所藏托忒文文献。

下面根据笔者在田野调查中所获取的资料为基础，首先叙述以往在新疆伊犁河流域进行托忒文文献调查的概况，其次以内容分类来介绍伊犁河流域额鲁特人民间所藏托忒文文献的种类，最后简述今后对其进行开发研究的展望。

一 在伊犁河流域进行的托忒文文献调查概况

伊犁河流域所进行的托忒文文献调查可分为以下三个阶段。

（一）20 世纪 50 年代的托忒文文献调查

新中国成立之后，率先到新疆进行文献调查以及收集文献的人是内蒙古历史语言文学研究所（今内蒙古社会科学院）的墨尔根巴托尔先生。在全国范围内，内蒙古社会科学院所收藏的蒙古文文献数量最多，其中有很多珍贵的古籍文献。这归功于道荣嘎、珠荣嘎、额尔顿陶克陶、墨尔根巴托尔等老一辈学者们的辛勤劳动和不懈的努力。他们走遍全国各地，搜集蒙古文文献，并把搜集到的文献收藏于内蒙古社会科学院图书馆。其中墨尔根巴托尔先生就是一位重要的代表人物。他捷足先登，走访了伊犁河流域在内的新疆蒙古族人聚居地，收集了大量文献。毋庸置疑，内蒙古社会科学院所收藏的托忒文文献大部分都是这一时期所收集的。

总的来说，墨尔根巴托尔先生等前辈们的文献收集工作是成功的。这样的评价主要是基于以下两点：（1）前辈们在政府统一领导下进行收集，并得到当地政府和民众的大力支持和帮助，由此，收集到了大量珍贵的文献资料。（2）以墨尔根巴托尔前辈为代表的文献收集工作者们，将其收集到的托忒文文献收藏在内蒙古社会科学院图书馆，不仅保护了这些文化瑰宝，而且为广大学者的使用提供了便利。在最艰苦的工作环境和条件下，把文献资料全部收藏于公共图书馆，无疑是一个正确的举措。前辈们的辛勤劳动着实让后人敬佩。遗憾的是，在十年"文革"的大动乱中，这一工作不仅被中断，而且收集到的部分文献也不幸被遗失。

（二）20世纪70—90年代的托忒文文献调查

"文革"结束后，被中断的文献古籍收集工作迎来了春风，再次被人们所重视，其相关工作也逐渐开展起来。

1982年6月15日，来自中国社会科学院民族研究所和新疆维吾尔自治区社会科学院民族研究所、宗教研究所、经济研究所以及新疆大学历史系的10位专家学者组成的考察队，在全疆蒙古族聚居区进行了54天的田野考察。这是"文革"后被中断的卫拉特古籍文献搜集工作得到恢复的标志，并取得了良好的效果。

1984年7月14日，国家民委成立了少数民族古籍工作专门机构——全国少数民族古籍整理出版规划领导小组。随着这一机构的成立，各省、市、自治区民委也先后建立了古籍整理出版规划领导小组。这一政府机构的建立，对少数民族古籍文献的收集、整理工作带来了新的机遇。自新疆维吾尔自治区少数民族古籍整理出版规划领导小组建立以来，该小组工作人员走访新疆各地蒙古族居住地，搜集了几百部托忒文文献，目前在国内官藏中位居首位。其中大部分托忒文文献都是在伊犁河流域额鲁特人民间搜集到的。

如同上一时期，此次文献调查工作也是在政府机构的统一领导下进行的，所以搜集到的大部分文献资料也都收藏在了国家政府机构的图书馆、古籍整理办公室及相关图书资料室里。与以往不同的是，本阶段资料搜集中也有少数个人的文献田野调查。

需要指出的是，在此期间，有些人冒充官方及个别领导的名义，在伊犁河流域骗走了大量的珍贵文献。有人拿走原本只给收藏者寄回了古籍的复印件，有人甚至音信全无。更让人无法接受的是，被骗取的那些大批珍贵文献到目前为止下落不明。甚至有些拿走文献的人早已不在人世了。他们当年拿走的文献最终命运如何？无人知晓，或无人作证。这些行为伤害了当地民众，产生了负面影响，对今后的文献调查工作带来了很大的不便。与此相比，在20世纪50年代，墨尔根巴托尔先生等老一辈学者们的文献调查工作风范无疑是值得后辈们学习的。

（三）21世纪初期的托忒文文献调查

如前所述，2000—2015年间，笔者在新疆伊犁哈萨克自治州昭苏县

（昭苏镇、洪纳海乡、乌尊布拉克乡、喀夏加尔乡、夏特柯尔克孜族乡、察汗乌苏蒙古族乡、胡松图喀尔逊蒙古族乡、阿克达拉乡、种马场、昭苏马场、农四师七十四团、七十五团、七十六团）、特克斯县（特克斯镇、呼吉尔特蒙古族乡、二乡）、尼勒克县（尼勒克镇、乌拉斯台乡、胡吉尔台乡、科克浩特浩尔蒙古族乡、军马场）、察布查尔锡伯自治县（八连、奶牛场）、巩留县（巩留镇、莫乎尔乡）、伊宁县（喀拉亚尕奇乡）等6县（26乡镇等）额鲁特蒙古族人聚集地，进行了托忒文文献田野调查。笔者的主要工作是，在收藏者准许的情况下，用数码相机或扫描仪，对收藏者提供的托忒文文献进行全面拍照或扫描。若主人不准许拍照，则以记录原文目录、文献大小、页数总数等最基本的方法收集古籍信息。

与20世纪50年代和70—90年代的调查相比，现代科学技术的发展给我们现阶段的调查提供了很好的条件。充分利用现代技术手段，记录和搜集文献，不仅便利也节省时间，而且可以多一种方式来保存古籍。

二 伊犁河流域托忒文文献的内容分类

1999年，北京图书馆出版社出版了由乌林西拉主编的《中国蒙古文古籍总目》一书。这是迄今编写的最权威的全国蒙古文古籍总目录。该部力作收入了500余部托忒文文献。如果不包括德国波恩大学收藏的托忒文文献缩微胶卷和20世纪后半叶的几十部抄本，其录入的实际数量也只有400余部。尤其遗憾的是，该书几乎全部忽略了伊犁河流域额鲁特民间所收藏的托忒文文献。

根据笔者搜集到的资料，伊犁河流域额鲁特人托忒文文献的内容分类大体如下。

（一）书信

目前，中国和俄罗斯是收藏托忒文书信最多的国家。俄罗斯对托忒文文书的相关研究取得了一定的成就。中国在这一领域的研究远远落后于俄罗斯。新疆维吾尔自治区档案馆收藏有"清代康熙皇帝赐土尔扈特阿尤西汗书"、"清雍正皇帝赐土尔扈特策仁敦都格汗书"、"清乾隆皇帝赐土尔扈特乌巴什汗书"等关系到18世纪卫拉特与清朝关系史的重要书信。此外，此处所藏卫拉特近现代历史有关的托忒文档案文书数量可观，内容丰富，是研究19—20世纪上半叶卫拉特社会历史最珍贵的资料。

除了新疆维吾尔自治区档案馆，中国第一历史档案馆、西藏自治区档案馆、拉卜楞寺等收藏着许多 17—19 世纪的托忒文文书。其中有 17 世纪卫拉特历史上赫赫有名的固始汗、噶尔丹与清朝往来的书信；1771 年带领土尔扈特部从伏尔加河流域东归的渥巴锡汗和他的属民与清朝往来的书信。除此之外，还有俄罗斯、哈萨克与清朝往来的托忒文书信。这些托忒文文献尤为珍贵。但遗憾的是，上述这些托忒文书信的统计、编写目录、影印出版、研究利用等工作尚未全面展开。我们期待 17—20 世纪初期这些托忒文文书早日公之于世。

伊犁河流域民间收藏的托忒文书信数量不多。伊犁哈萨克自治州特克斯县呼吉尔特蒙古族乡退休医生浩盖·根扎布（1949—　　）收藏着几份 20 世纪初期（民国时期）的托忒文文书。主要是寺庙喇嘛之间往来之信函。

（二）史学著作

俄罗斯和蒙古国是目前收藏托忒文史学著作最多的两个国家。中国藏托忒文史学著作不多，且主要为伊犁河流域额鲁特人民间所藏。

托忒文史学著作中最珍贵的无疑是《拉布紧巴咱雅班第达传——月光》（以下简称《月光》）。《月光》成书于 17 世纪 90 年代，由咱雅班第达弟子拉德纳巴达尔所撰写。该传记记载了 1599—1691 年，即咱雅班第达出生至圆寂以及他的转世灵童的一些生平事迹，其内容几乎包含了卫拉特人一个世纪的历史。《月光》除了记载咱雅班第达的一生以外，还记载了 17 世纪卫拉特的政治、经济、宗教、军事等方面的诸多内容。某种意义上可以说，《月光》是 17 世纪卫拉特历史的百科全书。俄罗斯和蒙古国发现了不少《月光》的珍贵抄本。至今在中国所发现的《月光》抄本仅有一部。该手抄本曾收藏在特克斯胡图格图库伦。"文革"初，艾拉德尔喇嘛把《月光》交给普塔，藏在胡鲁苏台之查干哈达。"文革"末期普塔又把《月光》重新交给艾拉德尔喇嘛。20 世纪 70 年代初，今伊宁市法院退休干部那尔麦·巴都玛，从胡图格图库伦艾拉德尔喇嘛处借走《月光》，但至今还没有还给原主。笔者曾多次访问那尔麦·巴都玛先生，但都未能看到该抄本。中国所藏的最珍贵的托忒文古籍之一《月光》，不知何时与学界见面。

佚名《准噶尔史——远古的历史》是我们近几年新发现的四卫拉特政教史。2002 年和 2004 年，笔者在伊犁河流域进行田野调查时发现了其四种抄本。分别由昭苏县二中退休教师巴音和希格先生（已故）、伊犁种马场力格希德·浩特勒特古斯先生（已故）、昭苏县乌尊布拉克乡医生孟和巴图先生三人收藏。在托忒文史学著作中，涉及政教史的甚少，所以佚名《准噶尔史——远古的历史》具有很高的文献学价值。

除上述两部史学著作外，还有德太《蒙古溯源史》。此书由伊犁种马场力格希德·浩特勒特古斯先生收藏。一直以来，学术界均认为此书是孤本，但在 2010 年冬季，我们又发现了其另一种抄本。

（三）语言、文学文献

在伊犁河流域，与语言学相关的文献不多，我们所发现的语言文献主要涉及托忒文的字母，有关转写梵文、藏文的阿里嘎里字的读法等内容。

比起语言文献，文学文献比较多。《江格尔》是蒙古族英雄史诗中最具代表性的巨著，其手抄本流传至今的甚少，它便是蒙古文学罕见的珍贵资料。在国际范围内，《江格尔》手抄本收藏的不多。迄今为止，伊犁河流域是发现《江格尔》手抄本最多的地域，而更让人振奋的是，目前在这一地区仍然保存着完好的《江格尔》手抄本。

此外，我们所发现的珍贵文学文献中还有 6 部《格斯尔》抄本。虽然蒙古学界对《格斯尔》研究已经达到一定的高度，但对托忒文《格斯尔》的研究，比如版本校勘研究等还需要进一步深入。伊犁河流域既有说唱《格斯尔》故事的艺人，又有《格斯尔》手抄本。这对《格斯尔》研究的进一步深入提供了良好的条件。

除此之外，伊犁河流域还保存着一部分祭词等文学作品。

（四）宗教文献

宗教文献指的是从藏文翻译成托忒文的佛教典籍。伊犁河流域额鲁特人收藏的文献中，佛教文献最多。迄今为止，我们在这一地区还没有发现与其他宗教有关的托忒文文献。

17 世纪初，四卫拉特盟主和硕特部拜巴噶斯汗率领四卫拉特的诸诺颜皈依了藏传佛教格鲁派。1648 年，咱雅班第达奉拜巴噶斯汗的长子鄂齐尔图台吉和次子阿巴赖巴图尔之倡议，创制了托忒文。咱雅班第达创制托忒文后，便开始带领其诸弟子进行佛经翻译工作。目前流传下来的绝大多数托忒文佛教文献，均属于咱雅班第达时期之译文。

伊犁河流域托忒文佛教文献不仅数量多，而且有很多珍贵的孤本。比如 18 世纪卡尔梅克木刻《金光明经》、1742 年木刻《八千颂》等等。

其中，伊犁尼勒克河岸发现的石经尤为珍贵。该石经是目前中国境内发现的唯一的蒙古文石经，在蒙古文文献中占有重要的地位。该石经一直到 20 世纪末期，藏在尼勒克河岸山坡上的岩石间。但现在已经严重散失，除一部分收藏在新疆维吾尔自治区博物馆外，其余部分都散落于民间。

（五）其他文献

除了上述四种托忒文文献以外，还有习俗文献和摩崖等。涉及蒙古族习俗的重要文献之一是与祭敖包有关的祭祀文献《查楚力音笔贴格》。伊犁河流域的额鲁特人不说"obuγ-a"一词，而说"degelin"（德格林）。"德格林"是蒙古语"上"的意思。这很可能是有关敖包的蒙古人古老而传统的称呼。但目前只有伊犁河流域的额鲁特人仍传承这一传统。"敖包"一词大概清代开始在蒙古语中广泛使用。那么古老的蒙古人是怎样称呼"敖包"的呢？伊犁河流域额鲁特人的敖包祭祀或许是最好的启示。祭祀敖包的时候，他们就诵读《查楚力音笔贴格》。其主要内容是首先召唤神仙，其次召唤准噶尔山水神以及诸汗。诵读《查楚力音笔贴格》也是伊犁河流域仅有的风俗习惯。伊犁河流域不仅收藏着大量的文献，而且保留着很多原始形态的风俗习惯，这些珍贵的文化遗产，有待学者们进一步研究。

天山山脉主脉深处的昭苏县阿合牙孜河谷洪古尔布勒克有摩崖。摩崖在阿合牙孜河南岸的巨石上。此摩崖由三个部分组成。第一部分是摩崖的中心内容佛教图案。佛教图案包括药师佛、吉祥八宝、吉祥如意等。第二部分则是文字。文字有两种，分别是托忒文和藏文。摩崖右侧有托忒文刻之三行六字真言，右侧上方刻有"药师佛"一词。藏文则刻在摩崖的中间部位，以四行重复刻了六字真言。第三部分是动物岩画。动物中有乌龟、羚羊、狗、牛等等。

阿合牙孜河谷摩崖题记字数不多，但有很高的文献学价值。目前，国内几乎没有发现托忒文岩文，而根据我们所得到的零星的信息来判断，即使有也已经被严重损坏。因此阿合牙孜河谷摩崖是迄今所发现的国内唯一的一座完整的托忒文岩文。

三 伊犁河流域额鲁特人收藏托忒文文献诸多之原因

伊犁河流域额鲁特人为何收藏了那么多的托忒文文献？笔者认为有以下几个主要的原因。

（一）抄写文献习俗

抄写是人类发明印刷技术之前的传统制书方法。即使是发明了印刷技术后的很长一段时间内，人类还是以抄写的方式来记录着他们的文字。抄写是人类历史上使用时间最长久的一种文献记录方式。迄今为止，传承下来的蒙古文文献中，手抄本是最多的。也就是说，抄写是蒙古文文献流传至今的最主要的途径之一。尤其是托忒文文献大部分都是手抄本。托忒文文献刊刻始于 18 世纪，而留存下来的不过几十部而已。因此，可以说托忒文文献也是主要依靠手抄流传下来的。

伊犁河流域至今仍保留着抄写文献的古老传统。抄写托忒文文献的缘由很多。额鲁特人以抄写文献的方式来祈求避免因果报应，避免干旱等自然灾害，以及为死者超度亡灵，为后代祈福。除此之外，也重新抄写严重受损的文献。因此，抄写文献不一定只是被限制在佛教典籍的范围内，其他任何内容的文献都会被抄写。

（二）请经习俗

当遭遇疾病等天灾时，伊犁河流域的额鲁特人有请托忒文佛经的习俗。请经者先到喇嘛处说明来意，喇嘛根据其实际情况决定到何处请什么经书。根据喇嘛的指点，请经者带礼物拜访收藏经书者。当得到主人允许后，请经者可将经书带回家中，供祭品。关于经书，也有很多要求和禁忌习俗。如：每逢吉日要点佛灯，每年至少诵经一次，晚间不能把经书带到户外，经书必须放在房间最高处等。另外，伊犁河流域额鲁特人民间有诵经习俗。若没有要诵的经书，需前往藏书者那里请经文。

（三）诵经习俗

伊犁河流域民间有诵经的习俗。但是诵经的不是僧人，而是有专门诵经的俗人。当地称这些人为"哈喇巴克什"。在伊犁河流域，喇嘛们诵的是藏文佛教典籍，而哈喇巴克什们诵的则是咱雅班第达翻译的托忒文佛经。在 18 世纪，漠南蒙古地区也曾经出现过蒙古文诵经现象，且流传至今（比如在包头市梅力更庙）。但不同的是，内蒙古的蒙古文诵经局限在寺庙里，而且诵经者是僧人而不是俗人。在伊犁河流域诵经时，可以是一个人，也可以是两三个人或有更多的人共同诵经。最多时十几个哈喇巴克什一起诵经。伊犁河流域额鲁特人民间诵经习俗非常独特，这种习俗目前唯独在伊犁河地区有保留。

伊犁河流域的额鲁特人抄写文献的习俗、请经习俗、诵经习俗等传统，对托忒文文献的传承和保存起到了一定的作用。在伊犁河流域尤其是昭苏、特克斯两县额鲁特人收藏的托忒文文献最多，其中昭苏县是中心地带，并且完整地传承了与托忒文文献有关的风俗习惯。额鲁特人的抄写文献、请经、诵经等这些传统习俗在很多其他蒙古地区几乎失传了。所以对此进行深入的研究尤为重要。

（四）佛教信仰

目前还无法确定四卫拉特人最初接触佛教的具体年代。正如前文所述，到了17世纪初，四卫拉特联盟正式皈依格鲁派。咱雅班第达传教活动很活跃的年代，即17世纪40—60年代，佛教在四卫拉特的传播达到了巅峰。

随着佛教的传播，佛教典籍的翻译也开始盛行，而且佛经与佛像一样得到供奉。伊犁河流域额鲁特人迄今仍然把佛像与佛经放在同处供养。他们把佛经尊称为"burhan"，蒙古语 burhan 为"佛"之意。可想而知，对伊犁河流域额鲁特人民间来说，佛经与佛像同等，均为佛教最高的崇拜对象。这些无疑对佛经的保护起到了关键的作用。

（五）蒙古人珍藏书籍的优良传统

游牧生活是否适合珍藏书籍？游牧生活是蒙古文文献散失的主要原因吗？游牧是蒙古牧民最基本的生产和生活方式，是蒙古人与大自然和谐共处的最大的体现。游牧并不是世人所想象的那种落后的、原始的生产和生活方式，而恰恰相反，它具有非常科学的内涵。因此，蒙古人在游牧社会中创造了属于自己的灿烂文化。

每个文明都有它独特的制书和藏书方法。据《史集》的记载，蒙古大汗的图书馆里，除了蒙古人自己的书籍以外，还保存着突厥等世界其他民族有关的书籍和档案资料，且具有严格的管理体系。外人甚至很多蒙古贵族也无法接近那些珍藏的珍贵图书。明人所撰《元史》也记载了同样的内容。1771年，伏尔加河流域的土尔扈特部东归是人类历史上罕见的悲壮大迁移。他们以失去半数人的代价回到了准噶尔，在此过程中，他们不顾战争和瘟疫的残酷和长途跋涉所带来的艰难，把自己的书籍带回了故土。额鲁特人在"文革"期间，将这些书籍珍藏在山洞等隐蔽处，避免被销毁，等"文革"结束后，又重新取回，珍藏在其家中。

额鲁特人珍藏书籍的优良传统一直延续至今。这也是伊犁河流域额鲁特人民间收藏托忒文文献多的另一个重要原因。

四　关于今后伊犁河流域托忒文文献研究工作的展望

伊犁河流域额鲁特人民间收藏的托忒文文献数量多、内容丰富，其中有不少文献是官藏所没有的孤本。因此，该地区托忒文文献的研究任重而道远。根据笔者长达十余年的调查来看，目前应做的研究工作有以下几点。

（一）编写伊犁河流域托忒文文献目录

目录是文献研究最基本的，也是最重要的基础工作之一。而编写伊犁河流域托忒文文献的目录是当今托忒文文献研究工作中，最重要的课题之一。中国是收藏托忒文文献最多的国家，但遗憾的是，中国藏托忒文文献的专门目录还未完成。尤其是伊犁河流域的托忒文文献，虽然数量多，且有很多罕见的孤本，但至今没有学者对其进行过全面的搜集整理。笔者通过这些年来的田野调查，正在着手进行伊犁河流域托忒文文献的目录编写工作，希望更多的人参与到此项工作当中。

（二）伊犁河流域托忒文文献的影印出版

影印出版也是文献研究中最重要的基础工作之一。只有影印出版才能给读者提供最科学的第一手资料。中国托忒文文献的影印出版工作还处于初级阶段。

（三）建立文献资料中心

伊犁河流域托忒文文献大部分散落于民间，对研究者而言，亲眼看到文献原件是非常困难的事情。另外，就目前的条件，我们无法影印出版全部托忒文文献。因此建立文献资料中心势在必行。学者们可以一方面继续在伊犁河流域民间搜集托忒文文献，另一方面可以利用数码照相机拍照的文献作为基础，建立文献资料中心，为更多研究者提供便利。

（四）制作缩微胶卷

保护文献的方法有很多种，其中制作缩微胶卷是一个很好的方法。2007—2009年间，我们完成了日本丰田集团的课题"亚洲周缘部传统文书的保存、集成、解题：新疆民间蒙古语传统文书的保存和集成——以伊犁额鲁特人为中心"。该课题是由日本岛根县立大学的井上治博士与笔者及伊犁河流域当地的学者、僧人共同完成的。其主要工作之一是把拍照的数码图片制作为微缩胶卷。我们在现阶段已经制作了1万张托忒文文献缩微胶卷。

（五）运用网络技术公开文献的图片

现在是网络时代，大数据时代。可以充分利用网络，在网上公开我们所拍下来的所有的文献图片，为研究者提供科学的文献资料信息。学者可以通过网络查看所有的图片，并且可以免费下载。若实现这一计划，可为托忒文文献研究者带来极大的便利。

（六）人才培养

20世纪70年代开始，新疆的蒙古族逐渐普及使用回鹘式蒙古文，到了90年代，均使用了回鹘式蒙古文。托忒文已经成为被淘汰的文字。在新疆，虽然有不少的托忒文出版物，但是新疆境内40岁以下的人们已经逐渐忘记了托忒文。目前国际蒙古学领域中研究托忒文文献的学者不多，尤其在中国，研究托忒文文献的学者甚少，因此急需研究托忒文文献的学者。培养人才是托忒文文献研究中又一个必须重视的问题。我们应该有计划地培养这类人才。

（七）进一步加强田野调查工作，继续搜集文献

伊犁河流域地形复杂、海拔高、气候多变，这一特殊的自然条件，给文献搜集工作造成了非常大的困难，给田野调查者带来了巨大的挑战。加之20世纪70—90年代，有人从这一地区骗走大量的珍贵文献，使当地民众对调查者持有很强的怀疑态度。因此，笔者没有看到的文献也不少，实际被保存的文献要比笔者已经搜集到的文献多得多。

除了托忒文文献，该地区还有很多回鹘式蒙古文、藏文、满文等文献。其收藏者主要以额鲁特人为主，另外也有少数哈萨克族收藏者。一些哈萨克族牧民在放牧时，在山洞等地发现了"文革"时期被秘密藏匿的文献，就把它带到家里收藏起来。"文革"期间，额鲁特人将文献藏匿后，因为时隔太久，有的当事人早已谢世，因而就再也找不到了。因此，在巍巍天山山脉深处，有可能还沉睡着不少托忒文文献，如果是这样，托忒文文献搜集工作就不能仅限于民间调查了。田野调查光靠个人的力量是不够的，必须由政府机构与学者联手完成。伊犁河流域托忒文文献的搜集工作是一项艰苦的和长期的文化保护工程。

（八）采取切实可行的文献保护措施

伊犁河流域额鲁特人收藏的很多文献已经严重破损，但是在偏僻的山区，无法用现代技术进行文献修复工作。当地民众只能将破损文献用透明胶、报纸、学生作业本等来修复，有些无法修复破损严重的古籍交给喇

嘛，而有的喇嘛则将其直接烧毁。因此，应该尽快采取行之有效的文献保护措施。文献保护工作仅靠个人的单薄力量是远远不够的，必须有相关政府机构对此采取切实可行的措施，才能避免更多文献流失和损坏。

在伊犁河流域，佛教信仰是古籍形成和传承的基石，传统是让古籍复活的生命力。迄今为止，没有任何一个蒙古地区像伊犁河流域额鲁特人一样，把信仰、民俗与古籍保存结合得如此完美。他们的诵经、抄经、请经、藏经等民俗，在深层次上已经具备了文献人类学的所有特点。伊犁河流域额鲁特人的信仰，为我们留下了更多的文字遗产。

此次影印出版工作得到中国人民大学国学院的大力支持。若没有中国人民大学国学院研究中国多民族文化的"大国学"思想，这些边疆民族所藏珍贵古籍文献不会如此迅速地见到广大读者。我作为此古籍文献的搜集整理者，代表自己，也代表伊犁河上游的额鲁特人，向中国人民大学国学院的领导表示诚挚的谢意！同时向中国社会科学出版社的编辑朋友们表示衷心的感谢。

祝愿民族古籍的研究和保护工作更上一层楼。

2015 年 10 月 21 日于日本东北大学东北亚研究所

Preface: An Overview on the Folk Collection of Clear Script Document by the Ölets in the Ili River Basin

The Ili River originates from the northern slope of the peak Khan Tngri, 6995 meters high above the sea level, the second highest peak of the range of the Tngri Mountains (Tian Shan) which play an important role in Central Asia. The river flows down like a proud dragon jumping from the sky, with the same majesty. Moreover, as it flows from the west to the east from Kazakhstan it reaches China after taking beginning of its main water from the glacier of the Tngri Mountains. In the upper part the river has three tributaries: the Künggüs (in Chinese and other languages also Kunges/Kunes), the Tekes and the Qasi (Kax/Kash), and they are like wrathful lions, galloping and snarling. When the Künggüs River going to the north joins with the Qasi River it becomes the Ili. The Ili River when going to the west joins with the Khorgus (Horgos) River and enters Kazakhstan again. In its lower part the river passes 3000 places including such ancient cities as Alimatu (Almaty) and goes to the Balkhash Lake where it finally rests.

In the upper stream region of the Ili live Mongols who are mainly Ölets of the Four Oirats (known as "a piece of marbled meat, a part of the Golden Law" ①). They concentrate in the Uyghur Autonomous Region in Xinjiang, in

---

① *Alaɣ miqan-u tasurqai. altan yosun-u kelterkei.*

the Kazakh Autonomous Prefecture, and in the following counties (*xian* in Chinese): Mongolküre, Tekes, Čabčiyal or Qapqal Xibe Autonomous County, Nilka, Tokkuztara, Yining, Korgas and Yining city (Kulja). There are two reasons for their presence in this place. With regard to the Mongolküre majority of Ölets, they are the remnants from the great massacre of Jungars who were destroyed by the Manchu Qing dynasty in 1755 – 1758. Those who live in other regions are Torguts who escaped the same fate in 1771 from Jungaria and Jungars themselves who survived purges and united with them.

Ölets who live in six districts of Mongolküre, in ten districts of Nilka and *šabi nar* of four districts of Tekes and Tokkuztara are Mongols of the upper stream Ili River.

During the time from 2000 to 2015, I worked there on the basis of the doctoral degree grant of the State Foundation of Social Sciences, a special grant of the State Foundation of Social Sciences, the grant of the Association to Develop Japanese Research (grant for co-operation of scholars from Mongolia, Japan and China), the grant for teachers of the Central University of Nationalities (Minzu University of China), as well as state and university grants for co-operation with foreign scholars.

I examined state, province and city registers, archives, museums, libraries and cultural centers and particularly private collections of many regions, including Urumqi, Khobogsair (Hoboksar), Altay, Bayingolin, Bortala and Ili of Xinjiang; Hailar, Ningcheng, Huhhot and Alasha of Inner Mongolia; three provinces of Northeastern China: Harbin, Mukden (Shenyang) and Changchun; Chengde of Hebei province; and in Mongolia: Ulaanbaatar, Uvs and Khovd.

As the most fortunate I regard my discovery that there was a very strong cultural influence to preserve Mongolian books in the regions as far as from the western border of Ili to the region of Kharchin Tümed, and I found work on this subject the most meaningful in my life. Deeper understanding of Mongolian intellectual tradition and Mongolian culture became possible owing to this.

It is not only an important proof that Mongolian nomads preserved books with love and care, treating them as precious, like gold and gems. They also impressed the world by creating a culture of numerous substantial books.

During my research fieldwork the most astonishing were the collections of mainly early books written in the Clear Script (*todu üsüg*) , kept by the Ölets living in the upper stream Ili River. Important places for preservation of books by the Ölets are: Mongolküre of Mongolküre district, Qaraganatu (Čerig-un Agta-yin Talabai) , sumun Ordubulag, Tugulčin Bulag, sumun Čagan Usun, sumun Šatu Kirgis, sumun Qosumtu Qara Usun, Saiqan Dugui, Egülder Mor-in-u Talabai of Ili, 74, 76-dugar Tuvan, Egülder Qonin-u Talabai, Tekes district and Gova city, sumun Qujirtu, sumun Ničügün (second sumun) , Čab-čiyal Ügerči (eighth liyan) , Sön Talabai, sumun Üliyesütei of Nilka, sumun Kökeqotugur, Köke Tal-a of Tokkuztara and Öi Šu of Yining County.

Some people keep two hundred books, and some keep over one hundred. The collections of those who have only a few dozens of them are not regarded as impressive. Here, Mongolian texts written in the Clear Script constitute a collection of over several thousand books and it is without any exaggeration a collection that is several times bigger than any of the official collections in China.

Among these texts there is *Altan Gerel* (Sutra of the Golden Beam) printed in Kalmykia at the beginning of the 18th century, which is the earliest blockprint of this text. There are also many other very rare and important texts, including the xylographic version of the *Naiman minggatu*, which is the Mongolian version of the Sanskrit *Ashtasahasrika-Prajnyaparamita-Sutra*. It was printed in 1742, at the time of Galdan-Tsering Khan and it is the earliest blockprint in the Clear Script kept in China. Until now, as far as we know, the Ölets living in the upper stream Ili River, are those meritorious ones, who keep the biggest number of books written in the Clear Script in the whole world.

Upon the request of two rulers of the Jungars: the eldest son of Bayibagas Khan, Vchirtu Tayiji (or Vchirtu Sechen Khan or Sechen Khan) and his younger brother, Ablai Tayiji (or Ablai Bagatur) , in 1648 Rabjamba Zay-a Bandi-da Namkhaijamso of the Shangkhas, belonging to the Gürööchi clan of the Khoshuds, who earlier had become a monk in place of Bayibagas Khan's son and went to learn Dharma in Tibet, upon his return, in the valley of the Chu

River, invented *todorqai üsüg*, i. e. the Clear Script, later called in short *todu üsüg*, which was a new Mongolian script.

The Clear Script was used not only by the Four Oirats, but it also became an important tool in foreign relations in Central Asia. Many scholars commented upon this fact so there is no need to dwell on it here again. However, it can be mentioned that the Clear Script was used mainly by the Jungars and Torguts who experienced similar fate.

The Clear Script, having been used for over three hundred years, in the 20th century had to face changes. In the 1920s the Russian Kalmyks and in the 1940s the Oirats in western parts of Mongolia stopped using the Clear Script and started writing with the Cyrillic alphabet. At the end of the 1970s the Oirats of Xinjiang in China were encouraged to use the Uyghur-Mongolian script and in the 1990s the Clear Script that used to be taught at schools suddenly ceased to be the subject learnt by the children.

Nevertheless in Xinjiang there were books, journals and newspapers printed occasionally in the Clear Script, but the Clear Script suddenly became the most recently abandoned among the writing systems used by the Mongols in the past.

Why did the Oirats of Jungaria invent the Clear Script? What was the reason they eventually abandoned it? Mongolian politics, religion and other connected factors may answer these questions.

Moreover, to truly learn and understand the layers covering secrets of this mysterious nomadic culture is not a simple task. The Mongols are not that simple. Mongolian nomads who achieved high living standard did not only continuously improve their script but they continue to do so today. And moreover, there are signs that they will do it in the future.

The script is said to be the most important agent of culture. Script besides its outer shape and the fact that it is a tool to maintain relations of one society with others, by producing each sound animates the entire ethnic culture, gives life to its skeleton, blood and flesh by becoming its soul and even more. Which script among those that has been used and which the Mongols are using has truly been approved by the Mongols themselves as scientific?

Nowadays scholars defend their own locality, each one their own, or say things from the position of their personal interest. It is regrettable that there are a very few who look on the problem from the higher position of the culture of Mongolian nomads.

Mongolian scholars should draw conclusionsconcerning the problem introduced here: change of the script, especially its good sides. They ought to examine this from many perspectives, such as history, culture, state and religion, society, language, science etc. in the period of several hundred years that have passed. But because this sort of work is very decisive, it has not been done properly, which is regrettable.

Wasn't it acultural loss that the Mongols have abandoned one script and accepted another? And if it was a loss, was it significant or not? Is it not one of the important tasks of our times to do research and review critically this unexpected deed of the Mongols who kept changing their own script!

When examining from the distance only within the last one hundred years or so the shift from the Clear Script to the Uyghur-Mongolian Script and from the Clear Script to the Cyrillic, and then from the Uyghur-Mongolian Script to the Cyrillic – how is it possible not to learn from historical experiences and not to draw conclusions and learn your lesson?

The Clear Script was not invented very early, however, among the scripts that have been used by the Mongols it comes just after the Uyghur-Mongolian Script. Documents written in the Clear Script have been preserved carefully in China, Mongolia and Russia. The number of preserved documents is second only to those in the Uyghur-Mongolian Script.

The Clear Script belonged not only to the Four Oirats living on the borders of the Mongolian world and thus should not be neglected. It should rather be seen as an important agent of the Mongolian culture. Monuments in the Clear Script are a significant part of the composition of the culture of Mongolian nomads.

The first scholars who did research on documents in the Clear Script were the 19th century Russian scholars. Yu. S. Lytkin, A. Popov, A. Bobrovnikov and K. B. Golstunski did a lot of work on the documents in the Clear Script.

Later, from the 1950s onwards also scholars of Mongolia did quite a substantial work. Academicians B. Rinchen, Tsendiin Damdinsüren and V. Tsoloo in the period of the 1950s – 1960s were the outstanding leaders in this field. In the 1970s G. Luvsanbaldan continued the work they had begun. Work of G. Lubvsanbaldan, collecting and preserving monuments in the Clear Script together with his research on the Clear Script and its writings, conducted on a considerable scale, became a very significant achievement. In China, from the 1980s, Qu. Batai, Erdeni, Altangerel and Si. Norbu directed scholarly work on the Clear Script.

It is very regrettable that due to different reasons in the 1990s studies on the monuments in the Clear Script were discontinued in many countries. However, at the beginning of the 21st century they began to reappear. One of the proofs is the series *Oyirad sudulul-un nom sang* (Library of Oirat Studies) which is published in Mongolia by the Center of Clear Script Studies.

Studies on the Clear Script do not concentrate solely on the research that was done earlier and could be predicted. The reason for that is the fact that along the western borders of China, in western provinces of Mongolia and among the Kalmyks living in Russia, there is a considerable amount of books kept by common people. They have not been included into scholarly research until now, there has not been a catalogue of these works and we may say that the work on them is starting only now. This is not to say that the study that has been done so far should be discarded. Furthermore, it should be emphasized that in the future research on these materials should definitely be taken into consideration.

Now I would like to introduce some of the findings of my fieldwork done on the Clear Script sources preserved in the upper stream Ili River. After that I will describe subjects found in the contents of the texts written in the Clear Script. In the end I will outline plans for further research.

Ⅰ. Survey of the fieldwork on the Clear Script documents done in the upper stream Ili River

It is astonishing how Oirats of the upper stream Ili River, one of the veins of Central Asia, preserved in their memory hidden truths of their history and culture: wise elders told me endless stories similar to fairy tales and legends. The upper stream Ili River used to attract scholarly attention like a magnet. However, fieldwork research on the Clear Script documents undertaken there since 1949 till today can be divided into three phases.

1. Research on the Clear Script documents in the 1950s

In the 1950s, when new China was established, scholars who went to Xinjiang to collect written materials were Mergenbagatur from the Inner Mongolian Institute of History, Language and Literature (nowadays Inner Mongolian Institute of Social Sciences) and Coyijungjab from the University of Inner Mongolia. The Chinese Inner Mongolian Institute of Social Sciences holds the biggest collection of early Mongolian texts with considerable number of important and rare works.

It is a direct result of persistent and enduring work of Jorungg-a, Dorongg-a, Erdenitogtaqu, Mergenbagatur, Coyigungjab and others from the older generation of scholars. They traveled all over the country and collected Mongolian texts. Mergenbagatur, who traveled to Xinjiang, is one of those scholars. His visit to the upper stream Ili River and search for books is still remembered by people living there. Nowadays those Oirat works that are kept in the Library of the Inner Mongolian Institute of Social Sciences are mainly texts collected by him.

Collections built by Mergenbagatur and others at that time were successful due to the fact that the local governments and people were not only directly involved in the work, but they showed their genuine support towards the project. Later, when the "cultural revolution" was on, these texts, and there were many, were kept secretly safe from destruction and in this way it was beneficial for the collection.

Collector Mergenbagatur, with his profound knowledge, knew well the value of the cultural heritage that he had amassed. He stored all of the collected items in the library. During the most difficult period those who had built the collection stored it in the library making it common property. It was an act of courage, responsibility and confidence that should be learnt from them. It is regrettable that during ten years of disorder of the "cultural revolution" some of the texts vanished from the library collection.

2. Search for the Clear Script sources from the 1970s till the 1990s

After the "cultural revolution" the work of collecting sources in the Clear Script started again. On the 15th of June 1982 Research Center on Nationalities of the Chinese Institute of Social Sciences and Research Center on Nationalities, Religion and Economy of the Institute of Social Sciences of the Xinjiang Uyghur Nationality Autonomous Region as well as the Department of History of the Xinjiang University established together a "Research Group on History and Society of the Mongolian Nationality in Xinjiang. " Within 54 days this group did field research on the lands inhabited by Mongols in Xinjiang. They had as their main objective creating a "collection of historical and religious sources and material objects of the Mongols in Xinjiang. " This scholarly investigation initiated assembling sources in the Clear Script following the "cultural revolution. "

On the 17th of July of 1984 the State National Affairs Commission established all over the country groups in order to lead the process of editing and publishing early texts of nationalities with small number of members. Also local Councils of Nationalities, prior to that or later, they each established an office. In this way offices set up by the state contributed to the work of collecting and preserving texts of nationalities with small number of members.

After establishing the office for editing and publishing texts of nationalities with small number of members in the Xinjiang Uyghur Nationality Autonomous Region, Batu and Galdan and other officers went across Xinjiang and collected several hundreds of texts in the Clear Script. Among them were many texts found amongst the Ölets inhabiting the upper stream Ili River region.

Qu. Badai, vice-head of the Government of Xinjiang Uyghur Nationality Autonomous Region, head of the Chinese People's Political Consultative Conference, Altanorgil from the Pedagogical University, Erdeni S. Norbu, vice-head of Xinjiang University, To. Badm-a. Tö. Jamsu from the People Printing House of Xinjiang, Buyangsig from Inner Mongolia University, Batu and Galdan of the Office of Editing and Publishing Texts of Nationalities with Small Number of Members in the Xinjiang Uyghur Nationality Autonomous Region are the main

representatives of this period. At the time of those studies research was conducted mainly under official leadership; however, individual people undertook
quite significant work.

　　Part of the material collected during this phase was placed in the collection
in a proper way. However, it cannot be forgotten that also quite a significant
number of rare and important materials was taken away and became private property of individuals, officials or leaders. These documents have not been publi-
cized, unfortunately. Only some documents while being taken away were copied
and copies were given to the locals. Some of the people who took the books
died. Now there is no way to learn which texts have been taken away. It has to be
stressed that as a result of this behavior, owners of the books that were taken
from them not only lost their confidence in scholars, but later it caused prob-
lems to the researchers. For example, in the 1950s Mergenbagatur conducted
his collecting work out of love and responsibility for his culture. However, some
people say: "Mergenbagatur arrived, cheated us, took our books away and
left. " This became a common phrase that united people. Quite often I myself also heard such sayings and explained that Mergenbagatur placed the books in the
library, and only a small number of them disappeared during the "cultural revolution," while all the others remained in the library. While doing work for the
culture one has to face people of all sorts of characters, egoistic or rude. One
not only has to study one's culture, but it is also a duty of man of writing to preserve and protect culture. But oppressing, hiding and making a private property
is not useful to scholarly work. And in the study of ethnic culture it is forbidden.

　　3. Studies of the Clear Script documents at the beginning of the 21th century
　　As it has been mentioned above, my fieldwork was done in the upper
stream Ili River in 2000 – 2015. During these fifteen years my main work was to
catalogue source materials preserved among the Oirats in Xinjiang. I used to take
pictures of every page, especially when staying at the foot of the Tngri Mountain, where I established my center of the four districts at the upper stream Ili
River: Mongolküre, Tekes, Nilka and Qapqal, and every year for a few
months I did my fieldwork there.

　　Every time I discussed with the owner of the text if he agreed that I take pictures of every page with a digital camera. If a person did not agree, I took notes about the biography of the owner, wrote down the text title and measurements of the book. My work focused on getting the approval of the text's owner. Even when I was offered to take the text with me, I did not do it as I decided to stick to strict rules. During the first two times there was a clear technical difference since in order to take photographs I used modern techniques of that time, namely camera and films and in this way the texts have been preserved till now.

Ⅱ. Monuments in the Clear Script kept at the upper stream Ili River with regard to their contents

The basis of my fieldwork was written monuments preserved at the upper stream Ili River. In terms of contents, these texts can be divided into several subjects, listed below.

1. Correspondence and legal documents

Correspondence and legal documents that are known to us till today are biggest in number among documents kept in China and Russia. Those kept in the Russian archives have been quite well studied or used for research. In the Historical Archive No 1 in China and Records Office (Dangsa ebkemel-ün gajar) of the Xinjiang Uyghur Nationality Autonomous Region as well as in several local libraries and archives there are still correspondence awaiting researchers to study it.

In the Historical Archive No 1 in China there are preserved important letters from the end of the 17th century and from the 18th century. In the Records Office of the Xinjiang Uyghur Nationality Autonomous Region there are three important documents connected with the 18th century history as well as plethora of correspondence dealing with the history of Oirats.

These documents have not been carefully studied so far by anyone and have not been used in scholarly works as source materials. In comparison with Russia and Mongolia there exist less historical documents written in the Clear Script preserved in China. Nevertheless, in China materials in archives and registers, which are connected with Oirat history and culture are not small in number and there can be found important documents among them.

There are not many letters among the documents in the Clear Script kept at the upper stream Ili River. What has been preserved is mainly correspondence circulating between monasteries and temples during the time of the Republic of China kept by individuals.

Collecting official documents and studying them have been rather thoroughly conducted by Java-yin Dusan from the Pedagogical Center of Tekes district in the Kazakh Nationality Autonomous Province.

He was able to ascertain that these documents had been preserved by Qoga-yin Qajab (b. 1949 –   ), a retired physician from the Qujirt Mongolian nationality sumun of Tekes district.

These arethe documents that were circulating between the monastery of Tekes Qutugtu (Teges-ün qutugtu-yin küriy-e) and the monastery of Ili (Ili-yin süm-e keyid). Eyilder, Qajab's uncle, was in the past a monk in the monastery of Teges Qutugtu and after his death the documents were passed to Qajab.

Moreover, in the private possession of Java-yin Dusan there are objects connected with Oirat history, namely two edicts ($\gamma asiq$, Tib. *bka'shog*) presented by the Fifth Dalai Lama to the Oirat temple. Also in the hands of Eligen-ü Osor from Bagurul Sagaralqan of Qaltagan sumun of Egülder Morin-u Talabai of the Nilka district there is one private letter written in the Manchu language.

2. Historical texts

There exist a considerable number of historical texts written in the Clear Script, preserved in Russia and Mongolia. In China there is a very small number of such historical works assembled in official collections. However, in the upper stream Ili River it was possible to discover several historical texts. Among these writings there is a famous text written in the 1690s called "Light of the Moon, the Story of Rabjamba Zaya Pandita" by Ratnabhadra (in short "Light of the Moon") .

It covers the life story of Zaya Pandita from his birth in 1599 till his death in 1662 and some events that happened in the period between 1662 and 1691 in connection with the incarnation of Zaya Pandita, the infant. It is a rare and important historical text that accurately describes religion, politics, economy and army of the 17th century. Several manuscripts of this text have also been found in Russia and Mongolia. So far we know that in China there is one manuscript of "Light of the Moon" kept by Kadar Narmai-yin Badm-a, who is a pensioner from the Kazakh Nationality Autonomous Province at the Ili River.

According to Java-yin Dusan this manuscript of "Light of the Moon" was kept in the monastery of Tekes Qutugtu. At the beginning of the "cultural revolution" Lama Anildar hid it with somebody he trusted in the Čagan Qad-a in Qolosutai and eventually it was recovered. In the 1970s Narmai-yin Badm-a went to the monastery of Tekes Qutugtu, borrowed the "Light of the Moon" manuscript and has been keeping it till this day.

The monastery of Tekes Qutugtu at the time of destruction in 1676 by Vchirtu Tayiji and Galdan Bushugtu was moved to the Volga region (Ijil jai) and also part of *shabi nar* (i. e. subjects) of Zaya Pandita are the people who established the Volga region. In 1755 they came from the Volga region to Tekes and settled down there. Manuscripts written in the Clear Script that were kept by *shabi nar* of Zaya Pandita are very important, and one of them is "Light of the Moon." But the fact that this valuable manuscript has been kept in private hands for over thirty years is very regrettable. It remains unavailable for scholarly work and for publishing.

The original place of an anonymous work, *Jegünγar-un tuγuji eng uridu aγsan uridu qoyar orosiba*, which is now becoming known to us and is an important text on Oirat religion and history, remains unknown. During my fieldwork in 2002 – 2004 I heard about four copies of this text. One was kept by Bayangsig, a teacher in the secondary school in the Mongolküre district (he died suddenly). Two copies were kept by Qotalategüs of Ligsid of Egülder Morin-u Talabai of Ili. One was kept at the collection of elči Čagan-u Möngkebatu of Ordubulag sumun of the Mongolküre district. Historical sources in the Clear Script that pertain to Oirat religion and history are very small in number. The text mentioned here, a very important source, was unknown until 1990.

In the collection of Qotalategüs of Ligsid besides the text described above, there is also a historical work entitled *Mongγol-un uγ eki-yin tuγuji*. In the past this text was not studied and has not been published in the form of facsimi-

le. This rare and important text was known only from one notebook, but last year
we found its copy.

3. Sources on language and literature

There are not many sources on language at the upper stream Ili River. The
existing ones are mainly handbooks of alphabet of the Clear Script, its transcrip-
tion as well as explanations and translations. Regarding literature, there exist
more texts than on the language. Two main representatives are great anthologies
of *Jangγar* and *Geser*.

Jangγar belongs not only to Mongolian folklore, but this composition is also considered an apex of poetry. There used to exist numerous manuscripts of
Jangγar, but now those transmitted in a traditional way are small in number. Manuscripts of *Jangγar* are valuable monuments of Mongolian literature. In
the past manuscripts of *Jangγar* used to be found at the upper stream Ili River. Nowadays some people still preserve them with due care.

Besides *Jangγar* in 2004 during our research in the Mongolküre district we
also took pictures of the *Geser* anthology entitled *Arban jüg-ün ejen geser qaγan
andulaman qaγan mangγus-i doroyiduγuliγsan ni*and *Arban jüg-yin ejen geser
qaγan-u tuγuji orosiba* and now we are preparing them for publication.

Furthermore, there are rare and valuable compositions which should be included in the history of Mongolian literature, such as *Galdan Bušuγtu qaγan-u
unal namanγilal* (Confession of Galdan Bushugtu), which is similar to the la-
ment of Togon Temür when he lost his city Daidu, ran away and recited the
confession of his sins. There are also other texts that have never been studied.

4. Sources on religion

Regarding the texts in this group, they are mainly translations from Tibetan. These are texts on Buddhism. At the upper stream Ili River we can find only
Buddhist texts. No texts on any other religion have been found. At the beginning
of the 17th century, under the leadership of the nobleman Bayibagas all Four
Oirats accepted Buddhism. As it was mentioned before, in 1648 Zaya Pandita,
at the request of two sons of Bayibagas, Vchirtu Tayiji and Ablai Bagatur, invented the Clear Script. The majority of texts that were traditionally transmitted
are translations from the time of Zaya Pandita.

At the upper stream Ili River there can be found many books written in the Clear Script. Not only are they not placed in official collections, but there also exist numerous authentically rare texts, such as *Altan Gerel*, printed in the 18th century by the Kalmyks from the Volga region. Other examples which should be mentioned here are the "Prajnyaparamita in 8000 Verses" (or in Sanskrit *Ashtasahasrika-Prajnyaparamita*), called in Mongolian *Naiman mingγatu*, printed in 1742 or the text of the Buddhist sutra carved in a rock in Čagan Qada (White Rock) in Nilka.

5. Other sources

Besides the four main topics of sources discussed above there are also sources connected with religious practices and rock inscriptions. When Ölets propitiate obo, i. e. sacrificial cairns, they prostrate and call it *tnger-e mörgökü* (to propitiate gods). During the propitiation of gods they produce *čučuli-yin bičig* (document of *čučuli*) and thus protective deities and local deities of land and water are not only entrusted but also many important mountains and rivers as well as land names are mentioned in the document almost without omission.

When relations are being established between parents of a new couple, there is a custom called *jogusu talbiqu yosu* (custom to set money). In this custom words are very meaningful. There exists a text called *yosu-yin üge orosiba* (words of the custom). Moreover, we can also find texts connected with such practices as starting the copying of a sutra (religious text), opening a sutra and others.

On the slope of the Tngri Mountain (Tian Shan) there is a cave in a place called Qonggorbulag. In front of the cave there is a painting on a rock and an inscription in the Clear Script. There is also Otači (or Medicine Buddha) painted there and animals such as a dog, a deer, a turtle and others. The inscription is both in the Clear Script and in Tibetan, it says " Otači " in the Clear Script and the mantra is presented in Tibetan. So far it seems to be the only known rock inscription in the Clear Script. We received reports about other examples of the Clear Script rock inscriptions in the upper stream Ili River, however, we did not have time so far to examine them and we plan to do it in future.

Summing up, it can be concluded that according to my estimation the upper stream Ili River is the region in which the largest world collection of texts written in the Clear Script (*todo üseg*) is kept in the hands of a small number of individuals, while the whole area deserves attention of scholars on Mongolian history and culture.

总 目 录

第一卷目录

第 一 卷

朝盖·古乃所藏
《能断金刚般若波罗密多经》

　　朝盖·古乃（1930—　　）　　新疆维吾尔自治区伊犁哈萨克自治州昭苏县昭苏镇额鲁特人。昭苏六苏木中的巴苏木人，大喇嘛额力根，离休干部，诵经者——哈拉巴嘎希，也是抄经者。收藏30余部托忒文古籍文献。

　　《能断金刚般若波罗密多经》　（《xutuqtu byiligiyin činadu kürüqsen tasulaqči očir kemekü yeke külgüni sudur orošiboi》）　　17世纪中叶卫拉特高僧咱雅班第达之译经。清代末期土尔扈特汗廷所木刻，土尔扈特汗布彦蒙库以及额吉福晋色日德毕力嘎德等作为施主倡议。10×36cm，41叶（双面）。除朝盖·古乃老人之外，尼勒克县医生巴特嘎收藏一部。

　　《能断金刚般若波罗密多经》是大乘佛教的重要典籍之一。在伊犁河流域额鲁特人民间，迄今为死者超度灵魂而诵，是托忒文文献中最普及的佛经，其木刻为最多，目前我们发现9种该经书的不同木刻本。

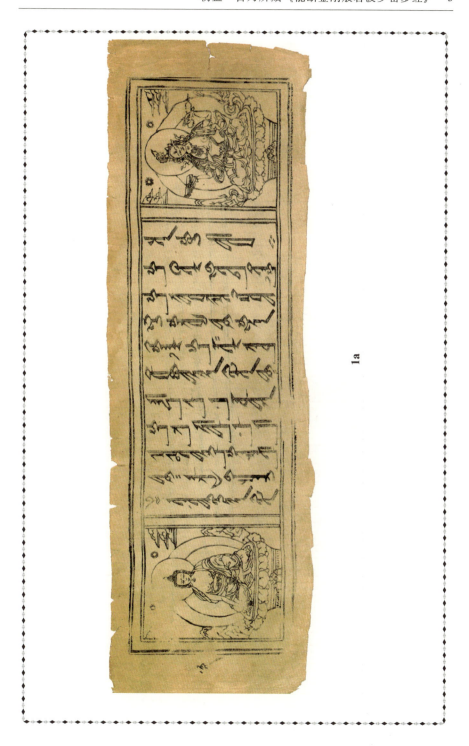

1a

2a

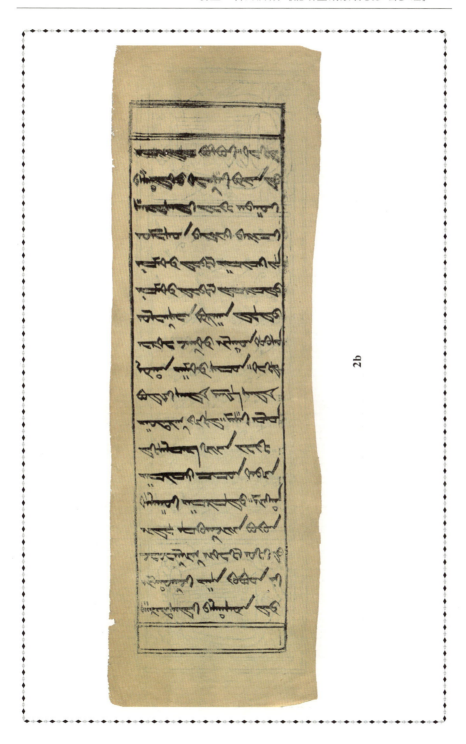

2b

3a

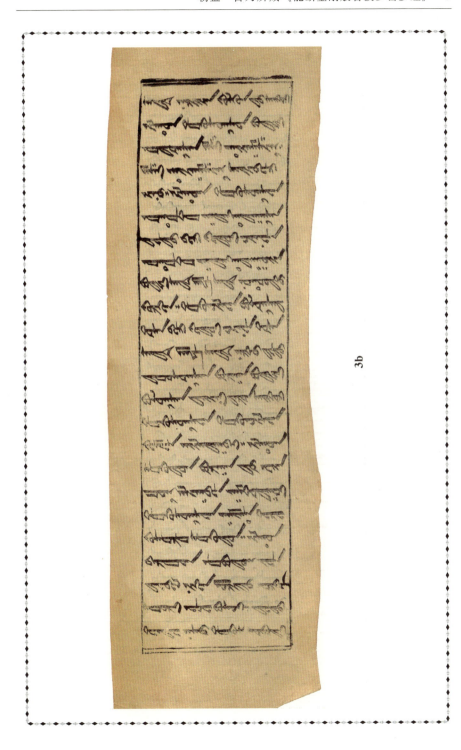

3b

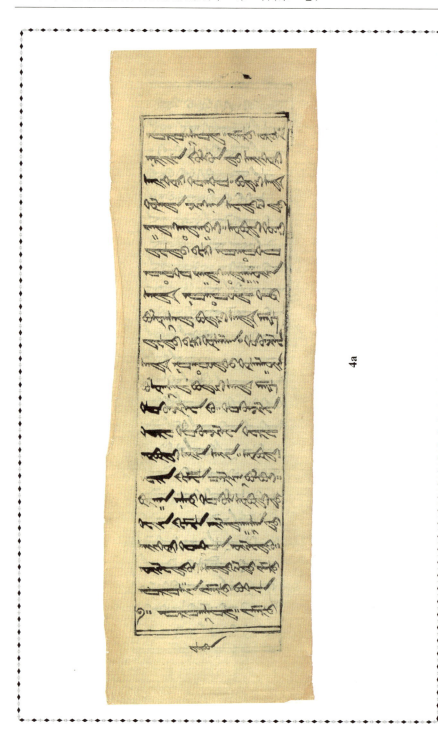

4a

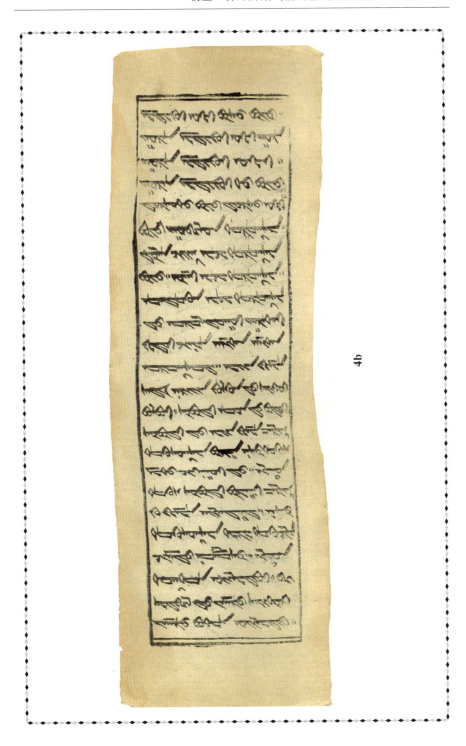

4b

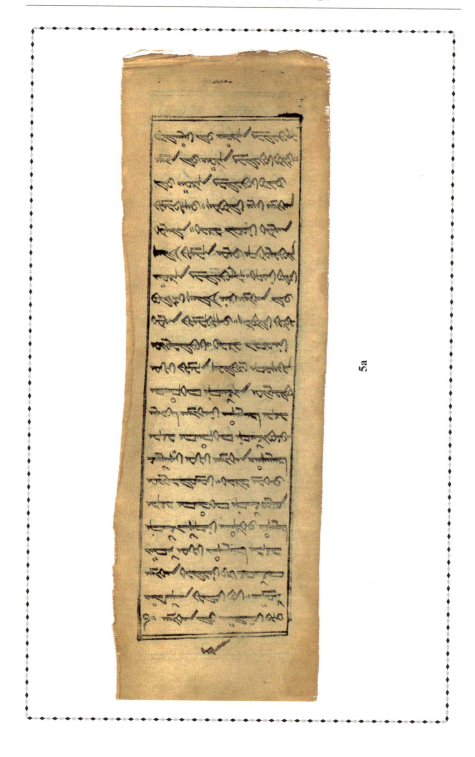

5a

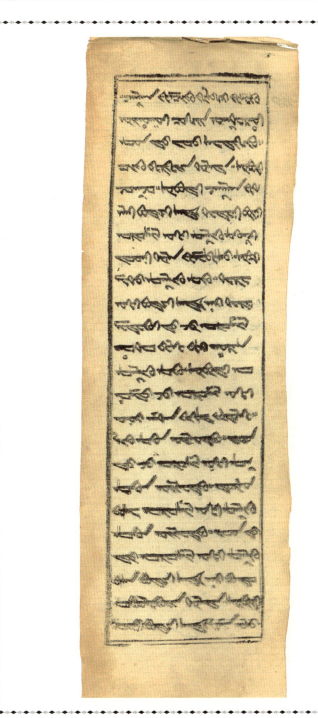

5b

6a

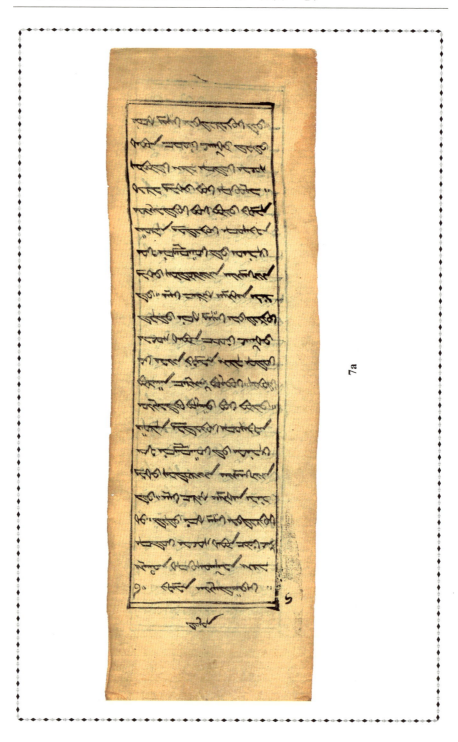

7a

7b

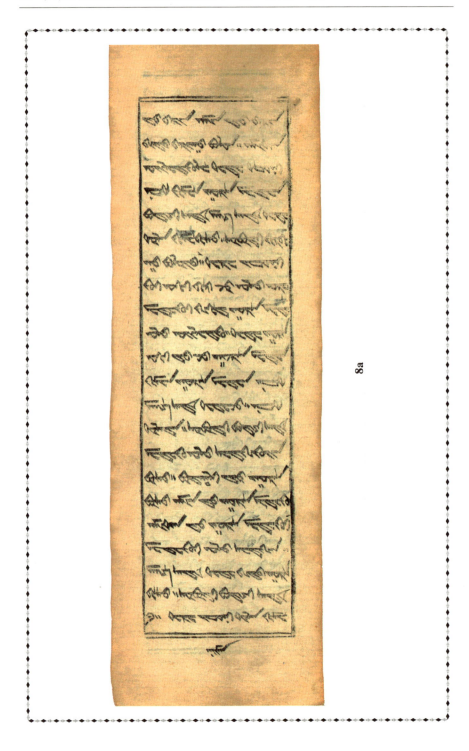

8a

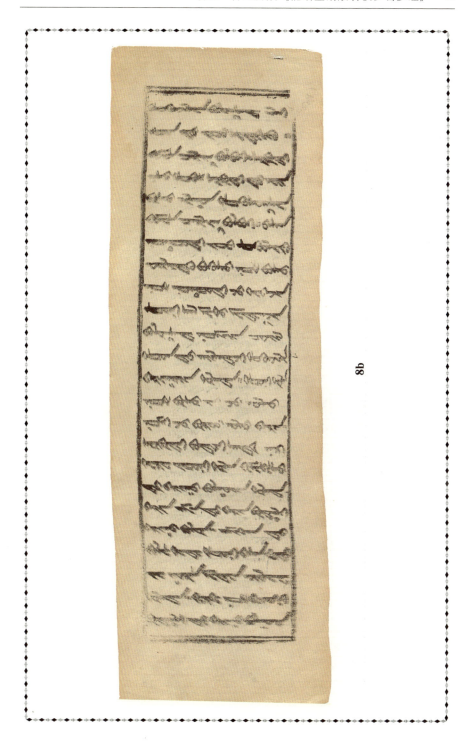

8b

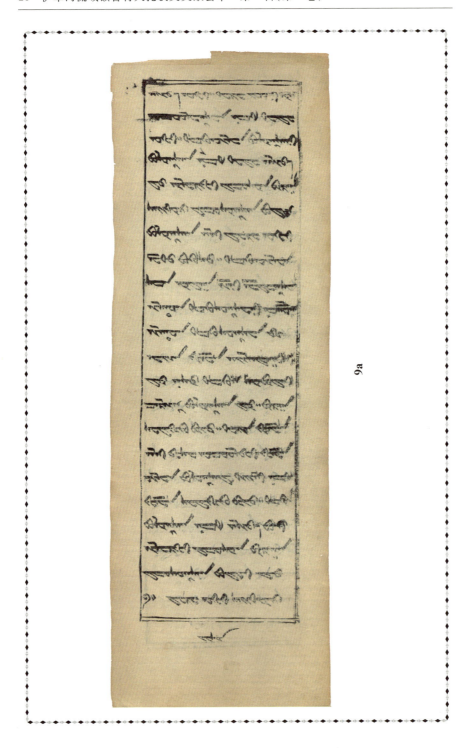

9a

9b

10a

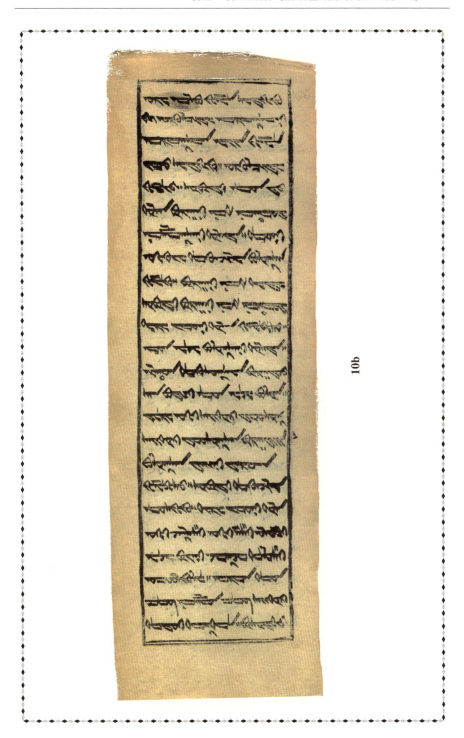

10b

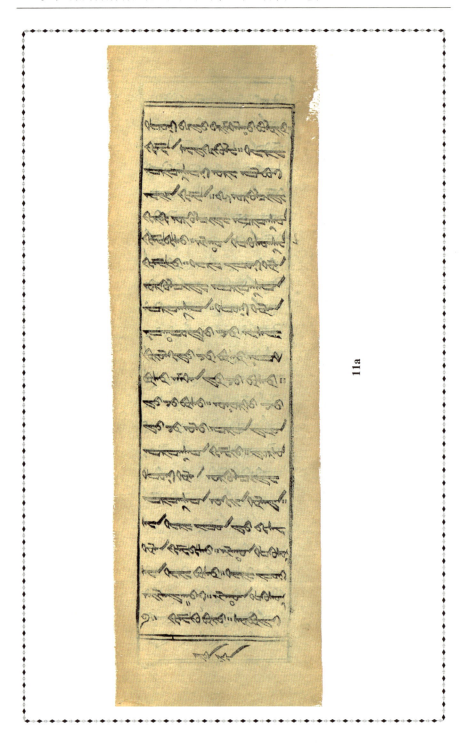

11a

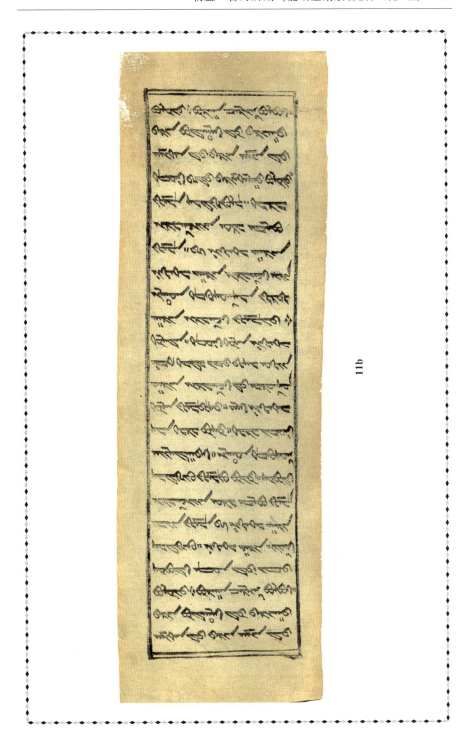

11b

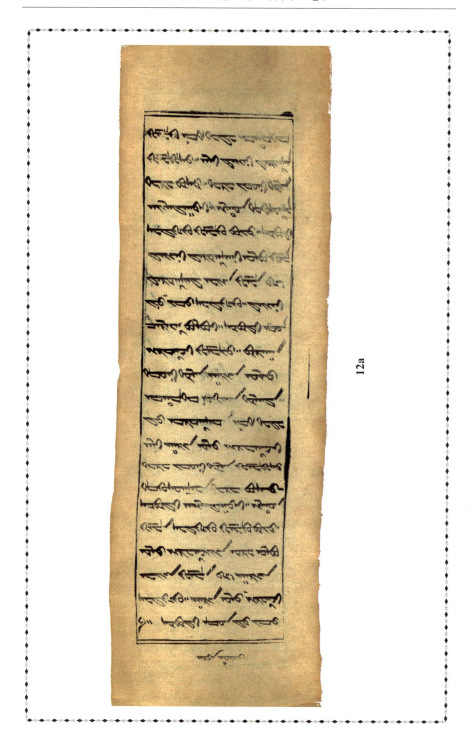

12a

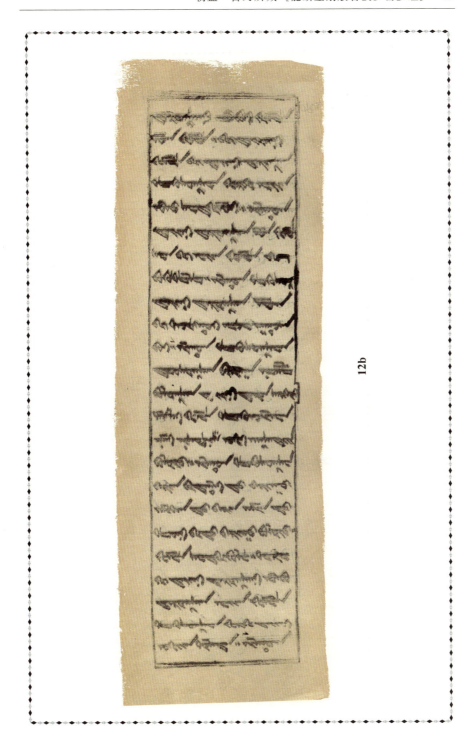

12b

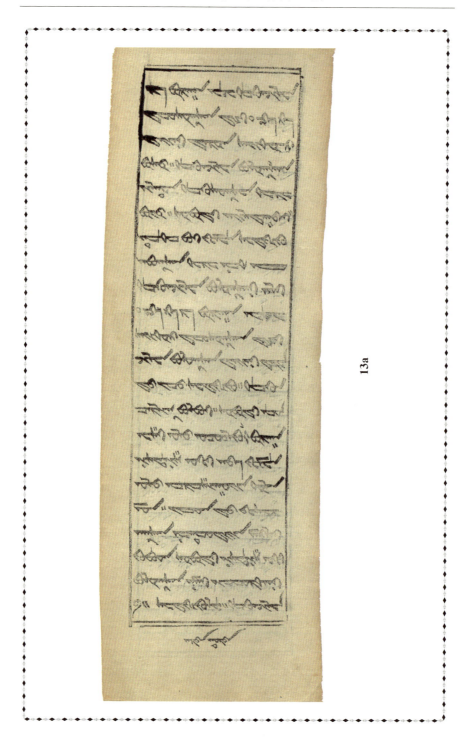

13a

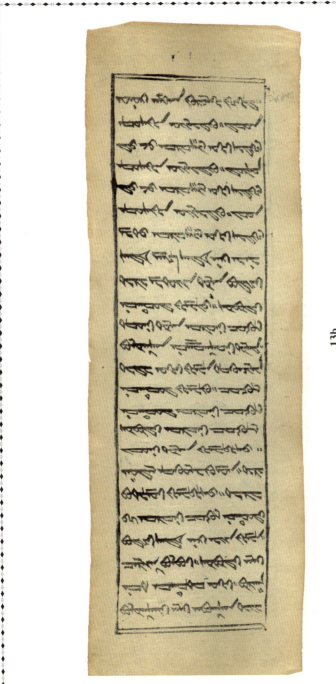

13b

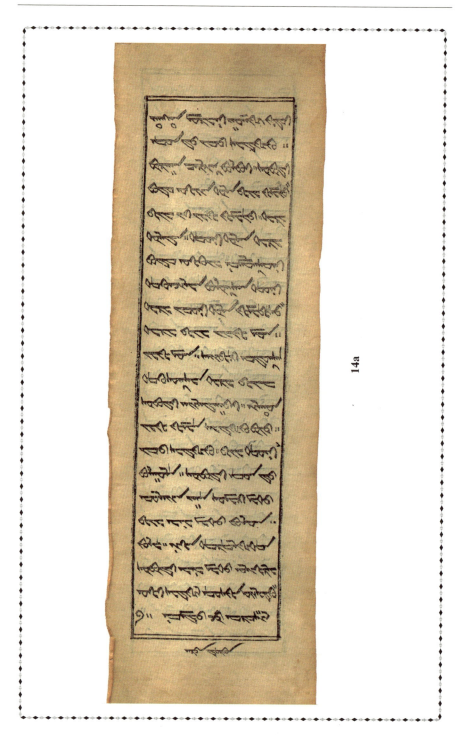

14a

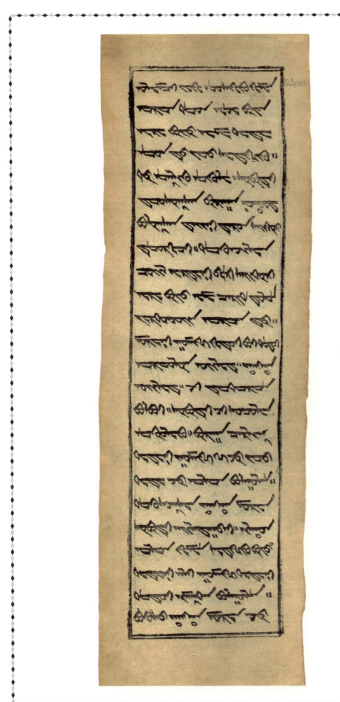

14b

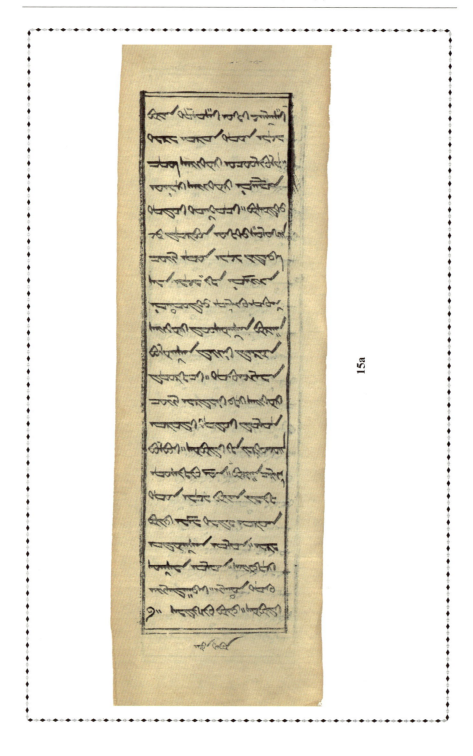

15a

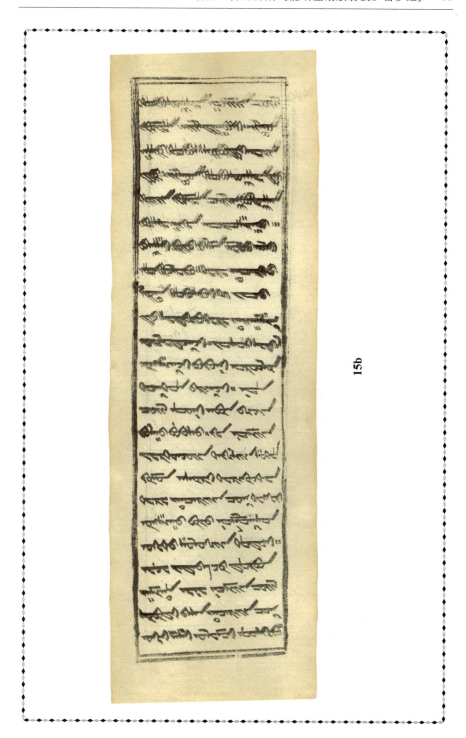

15b

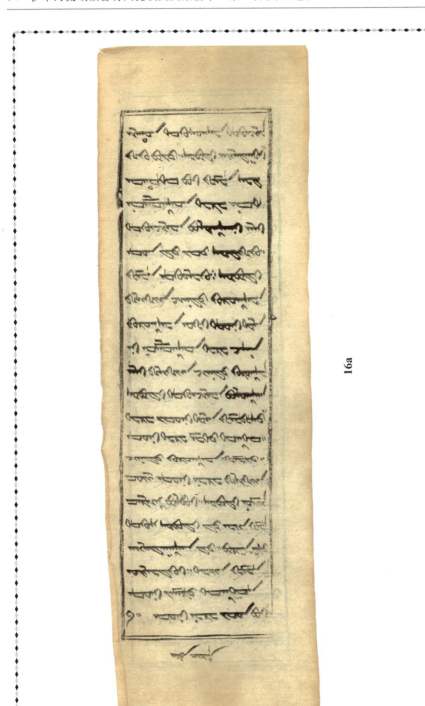

16a

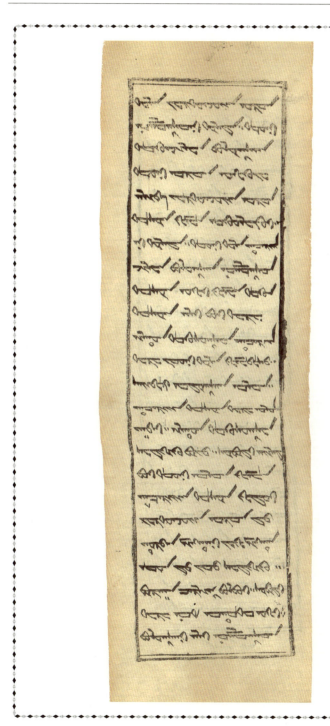

16b

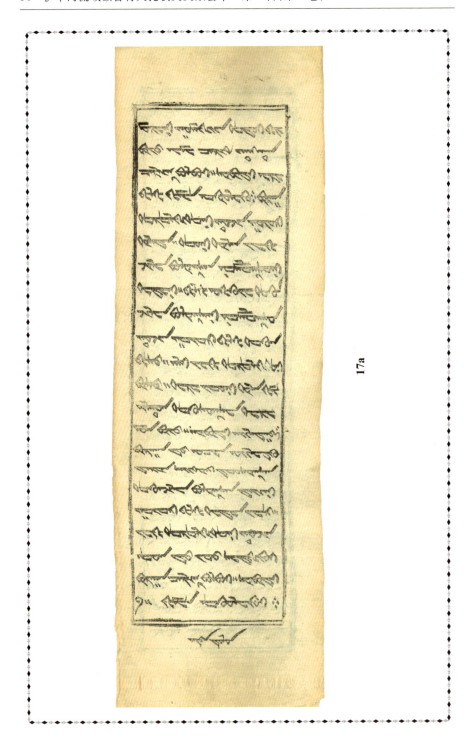

17a

17b

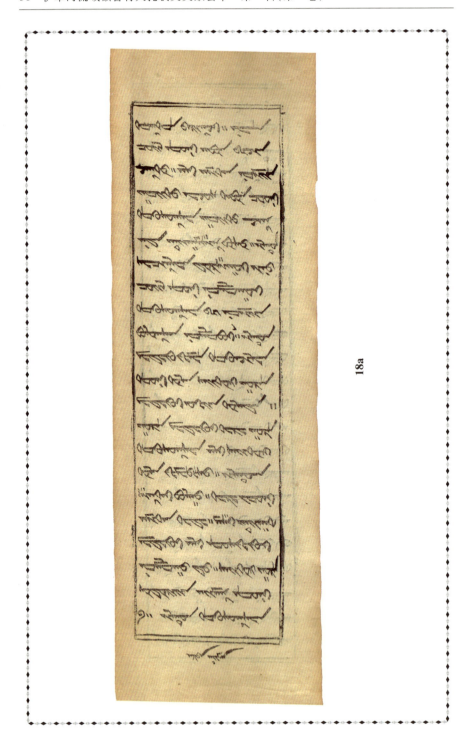

18a

18b

19a

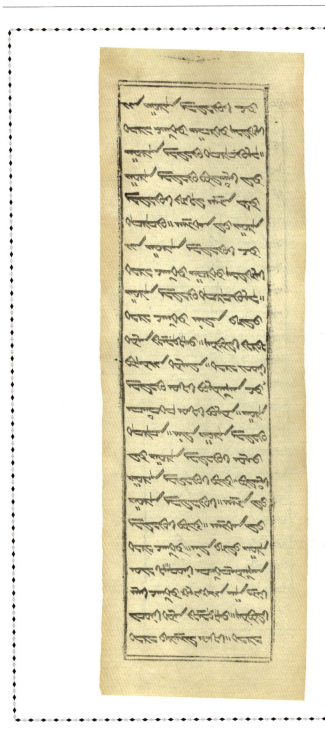

19b

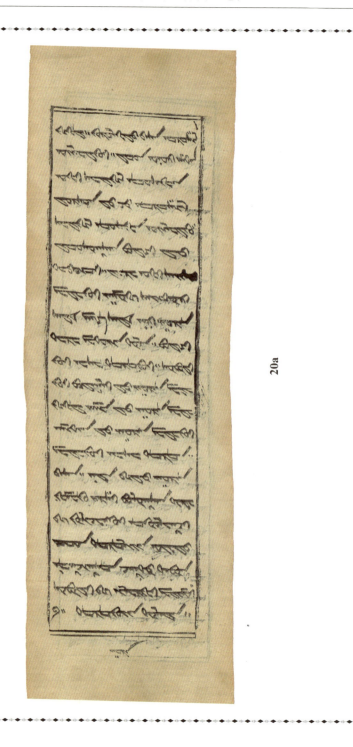

20a

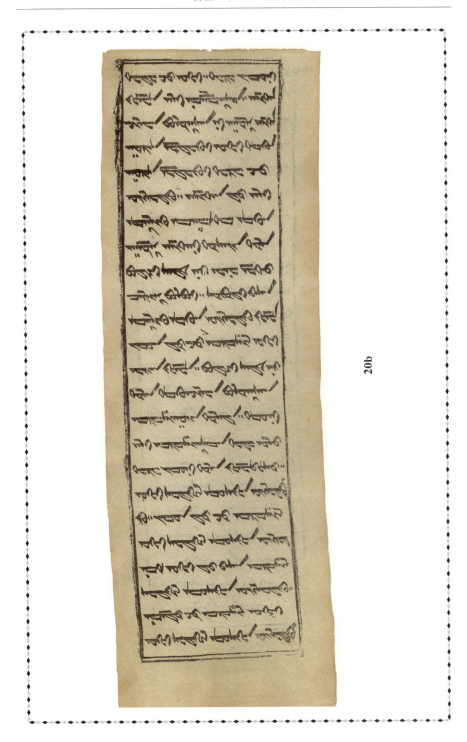

20b

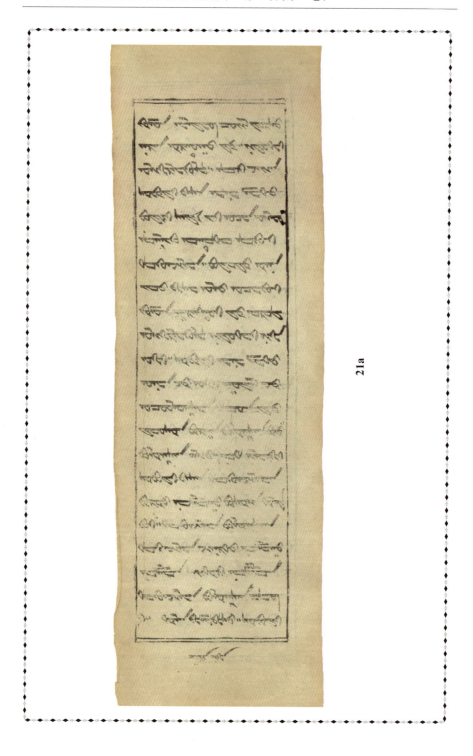

21a

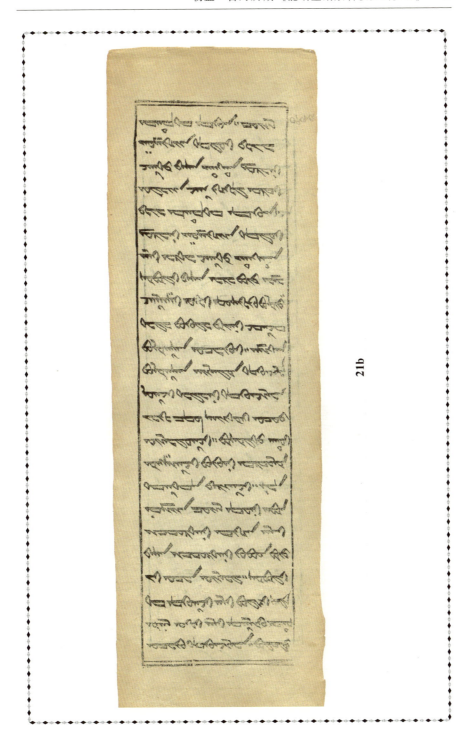

21b

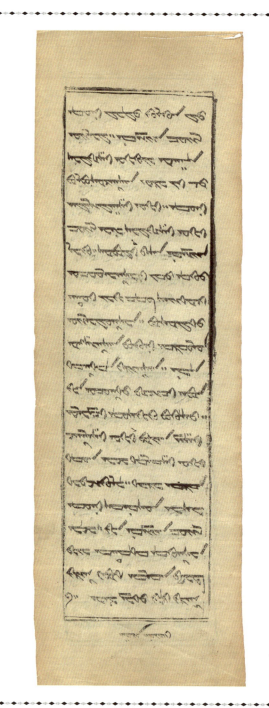

22a

22b

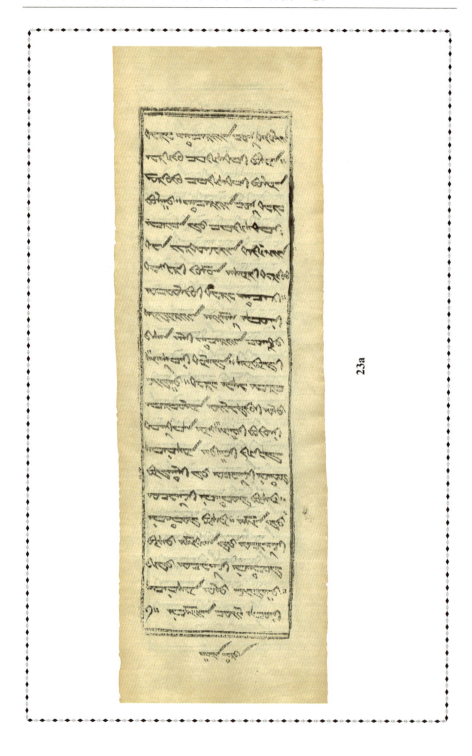

23a

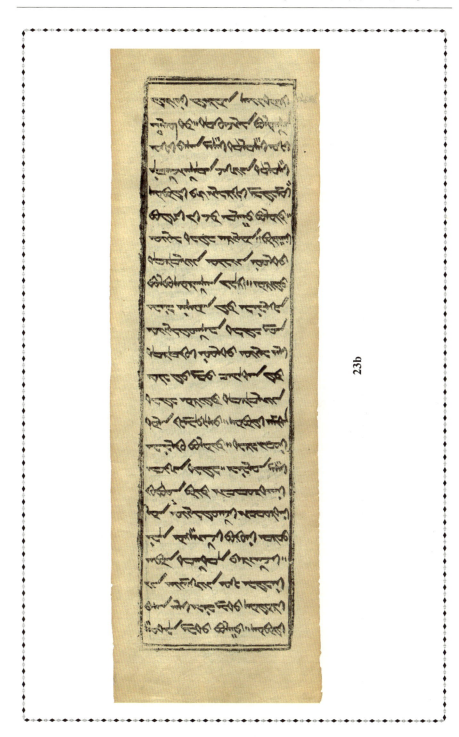

23b

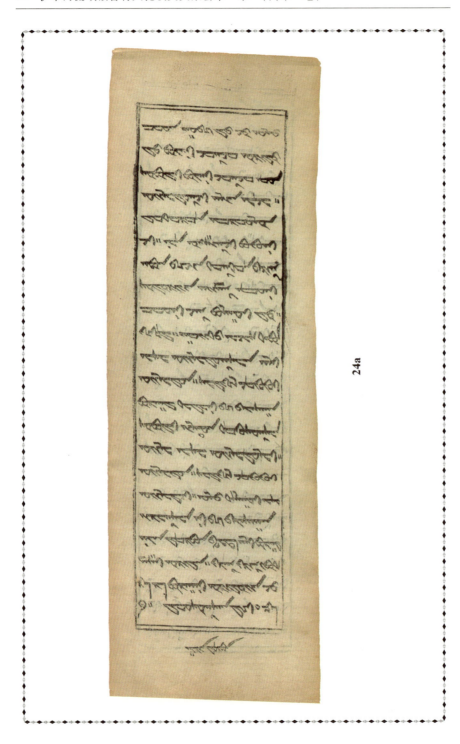

24a

24b

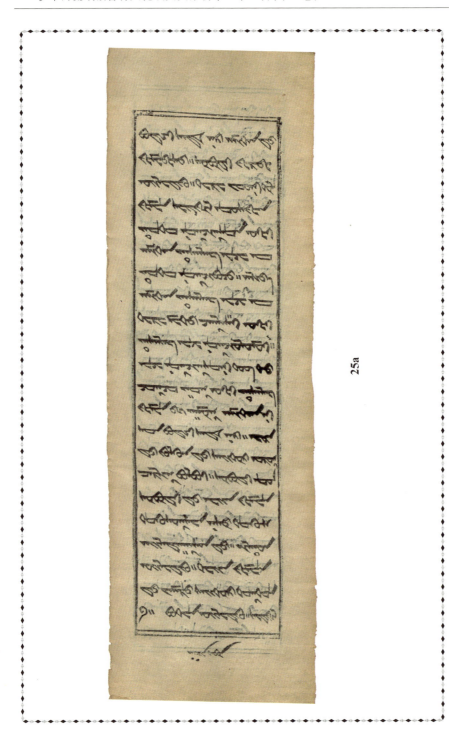

25a

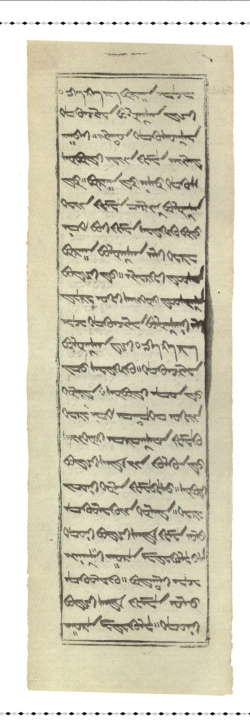

25b

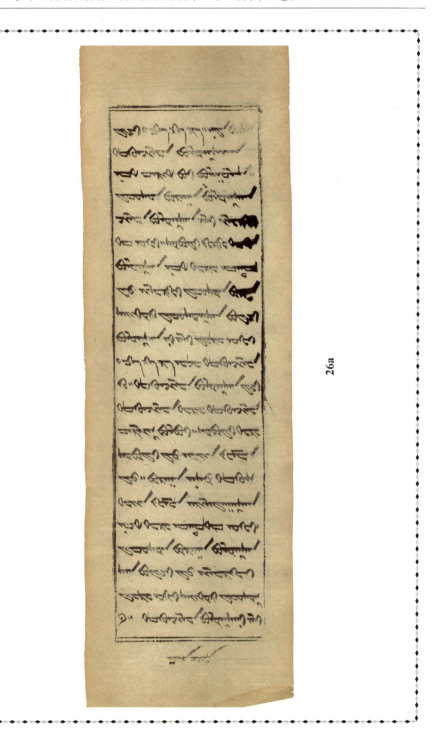

26a

26b

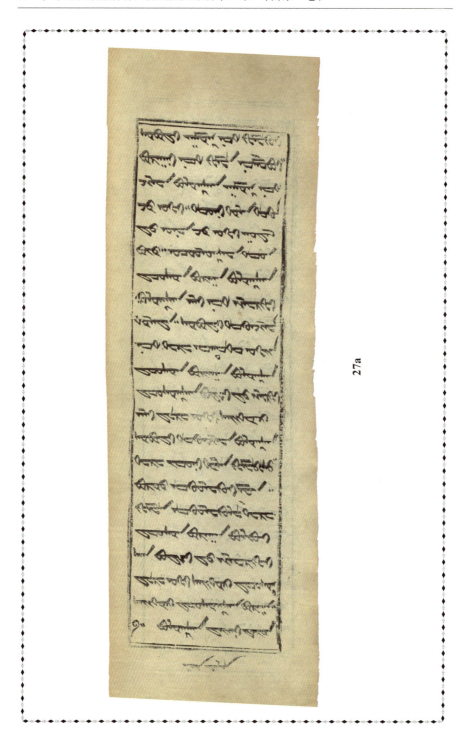

27a

27b

28a

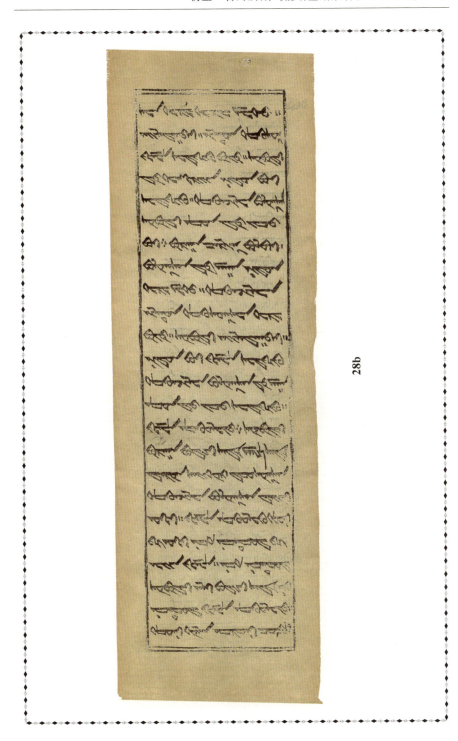

28b

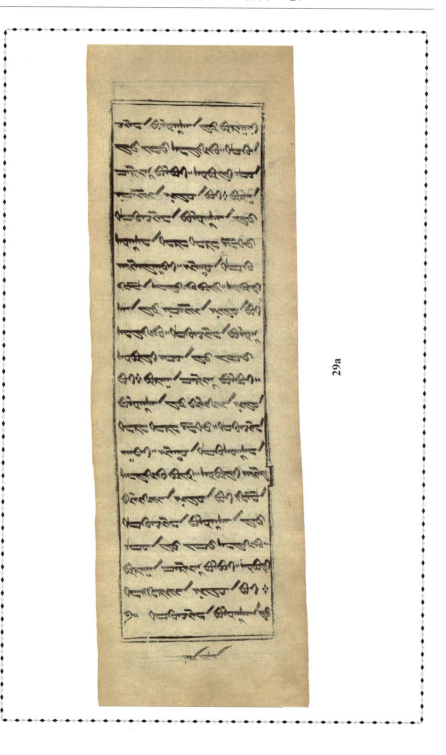

29a

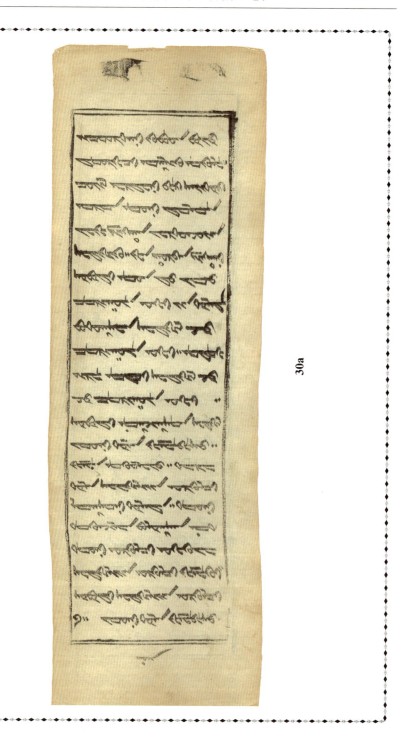

30a

30b

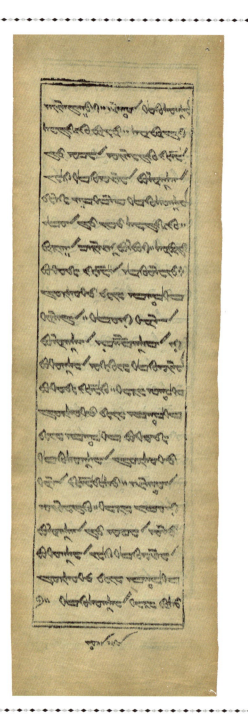

31a

31b

32a

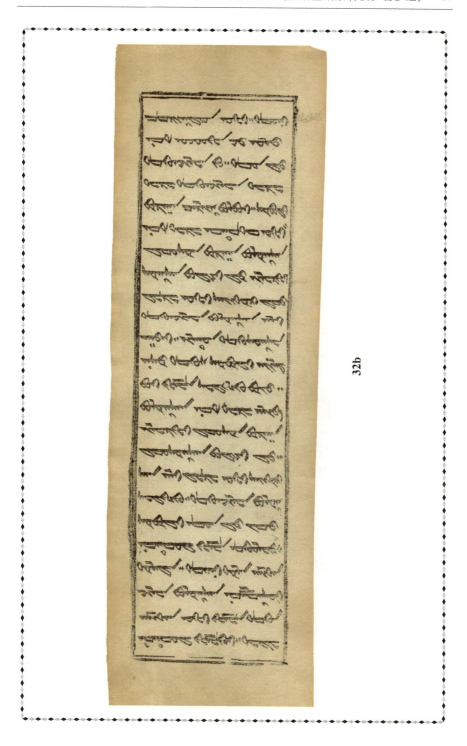

32b

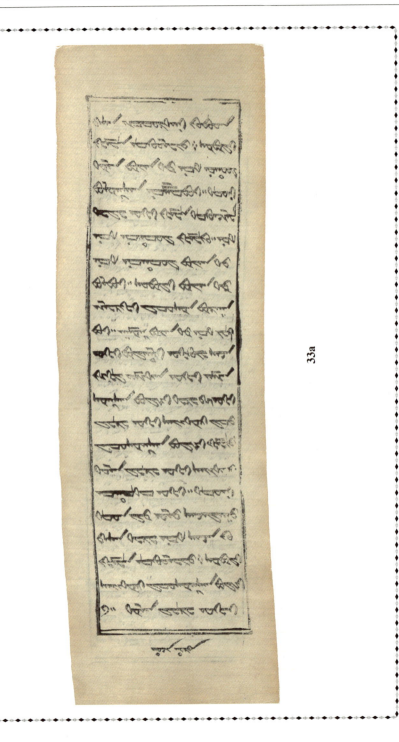

33a

33b

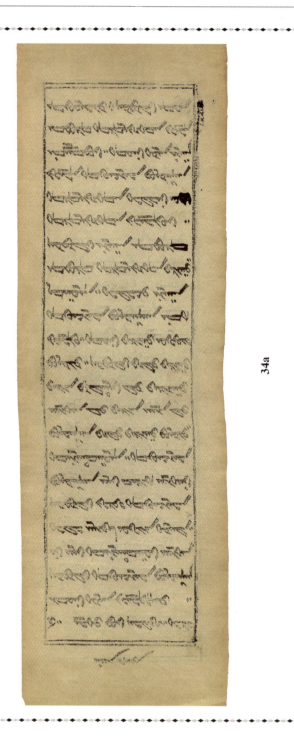

34a

34b

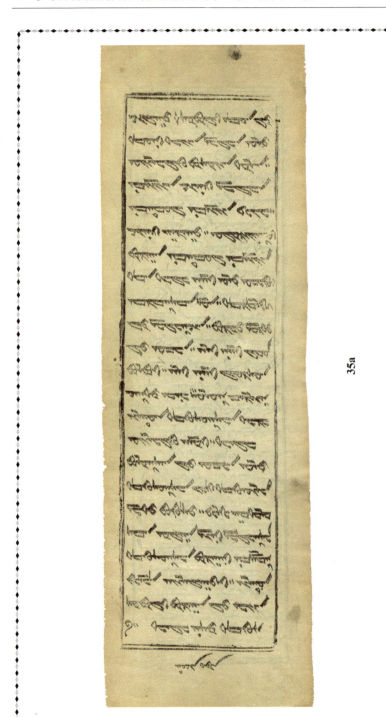

35a

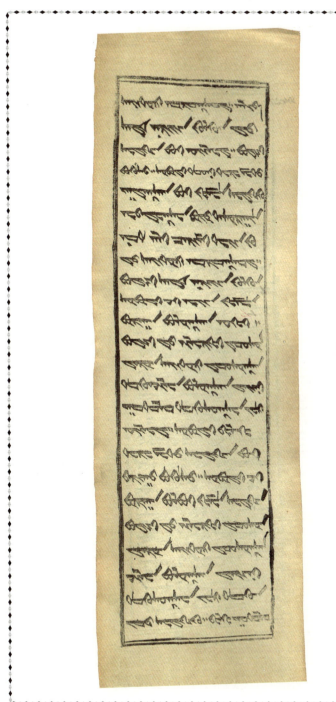

35b

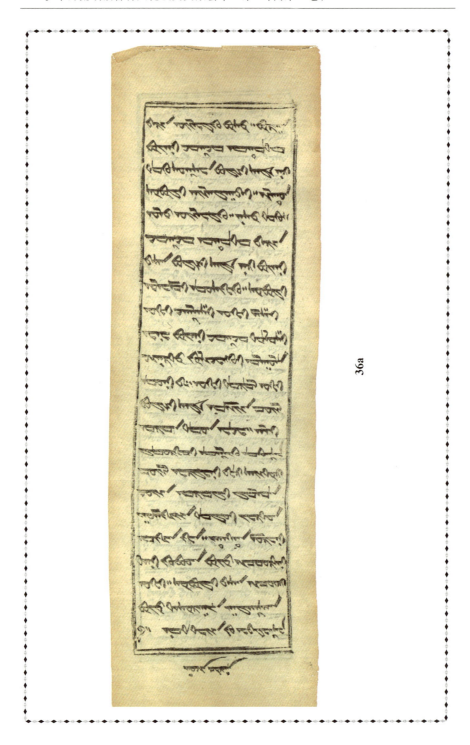

36a

36b

37a

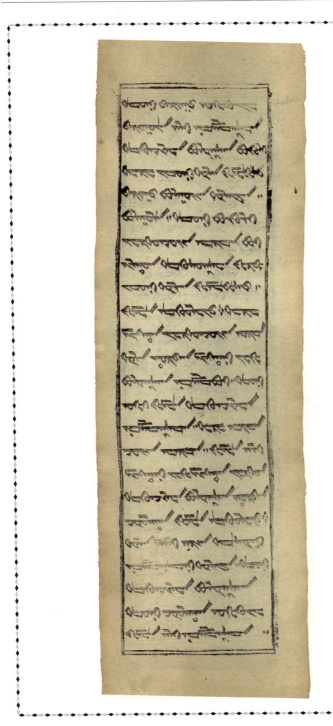

37b

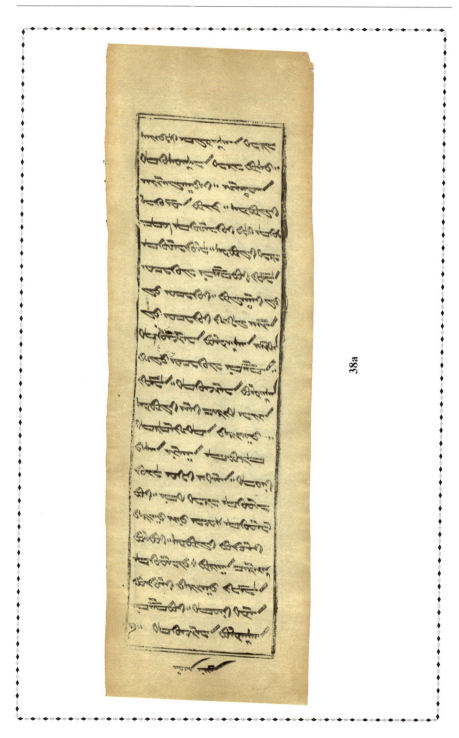

38a

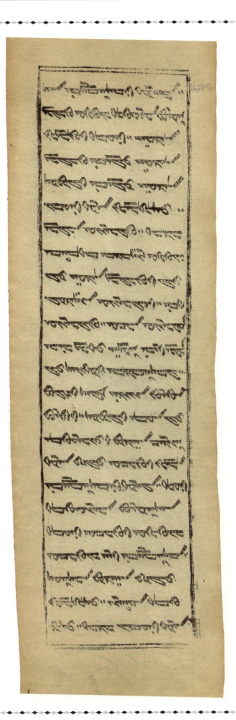

38b

39a

39b

40a

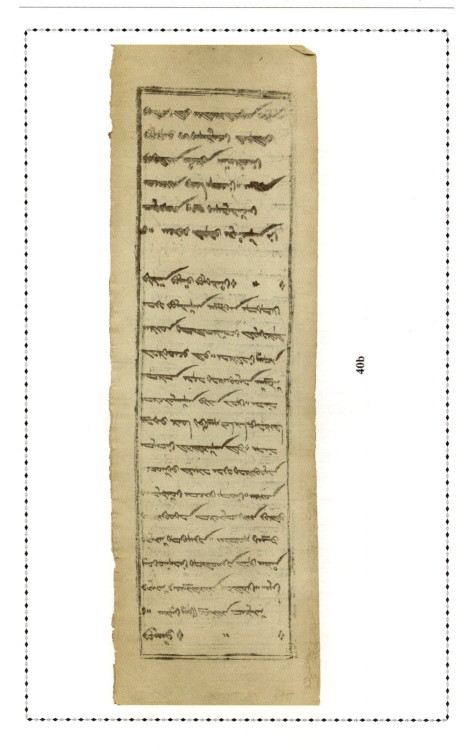

40b

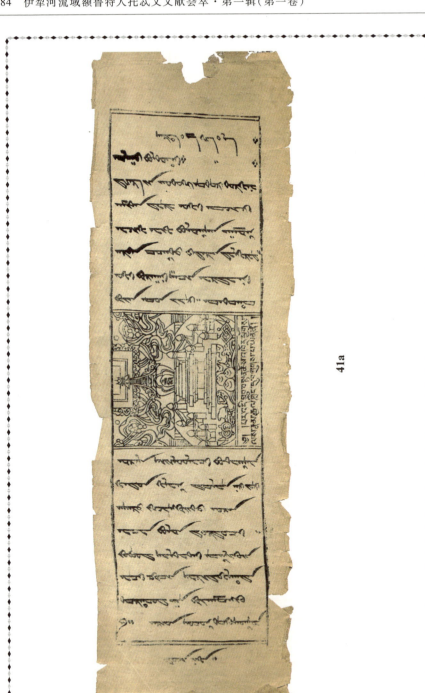

41a

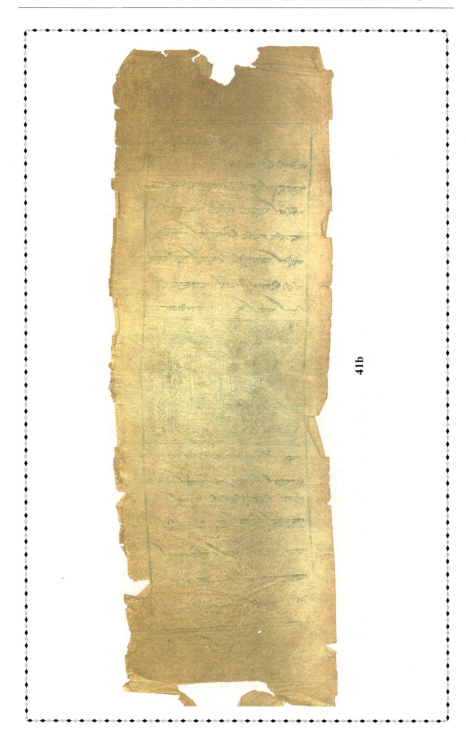

41b

巴雅斯夫喇嘛所藏
《能断金刚般若波罗密多经》

　　巴雅斯夫喇嘛（1973—　）　　新疆维吾尔自治区伊犁哈萨克自治州察布查尔锡伯族自治县奶牛场额鲁特人。昭苏六苏木中的托苏木人，查黑日玛根额力根。收藏30余部托忒文古籍文献。

　　《能断金刚般若波罗密多经》　（《xutuqtu byiligiyin činadu kürüqsen tasulaqči očir kemekü yeke külgüni sudur orošiboi》）　　17世纪中叶卫拉特高僧咱雅班第达之译经。1927年，在孟和杰倡议下，嘎拉仓、罗布仓木刻，是伊犁地区木刻，11×35.4cm，30叶（双面）。此部木刻在伊犁河流域流传广泛。昭苏县天山乡和硕特·浩士嘎收藏两部，特克斯县呼吉尔特蒙古乡额布勒锦喇嘛、昭苏县昭苏镇赛力木·苏布赛、伊犁种马场朱扎·巴雅尔台等各藏一部。

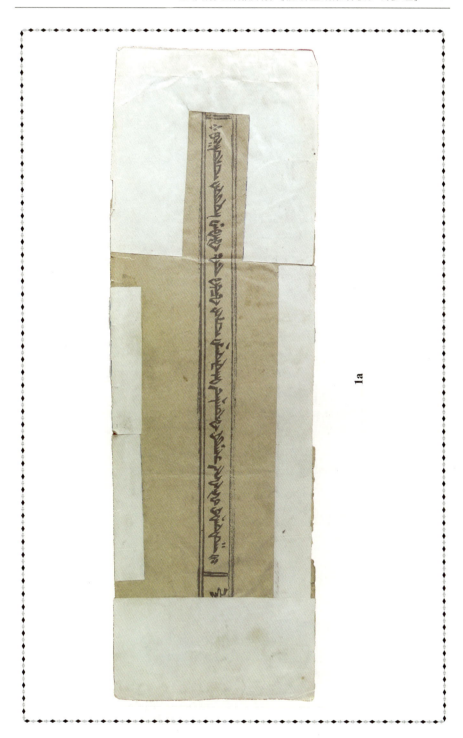

1a

1b

2a

2b

3a

3b

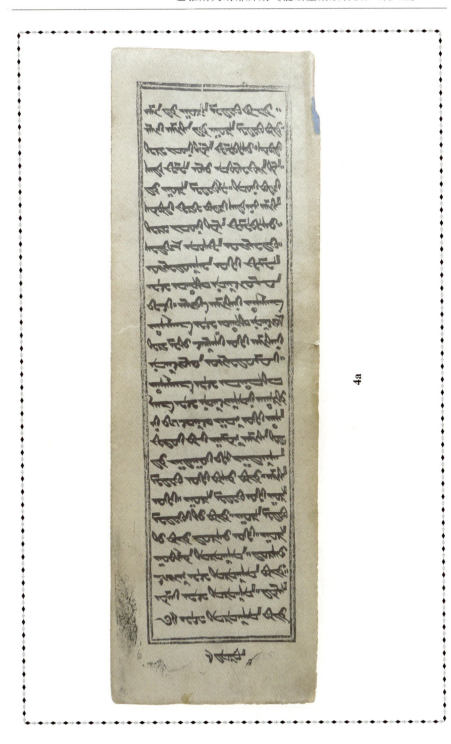

4a

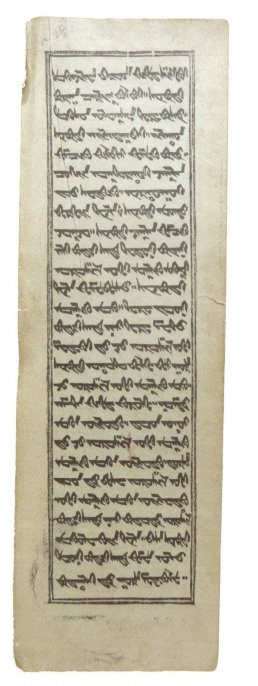

4b

5a

5b

6a

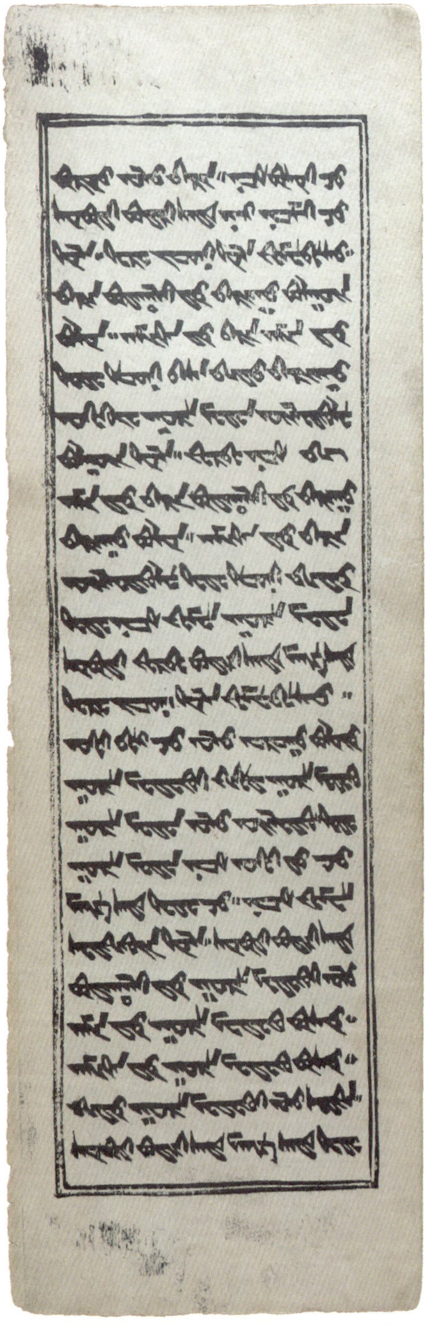

6b

7a

7b

8a

8b

9a

9b

10a

10b

11a

11b

12a

12b

13a

13b

14a

14b

15a

15b

16a

16b

17a

17b

18a

18b

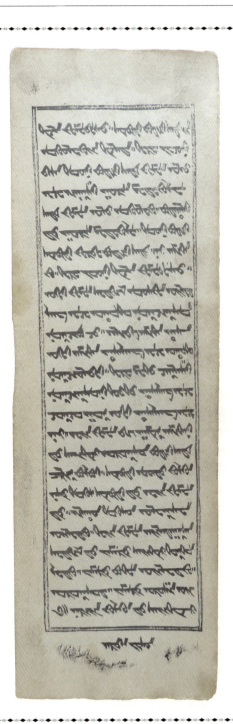

19a

19b

20a

20b

21a

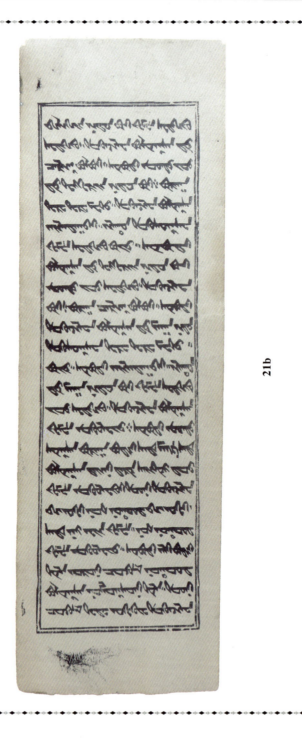

21b

22a

22b

23a

23b

24a

24b

25a

25b

26a

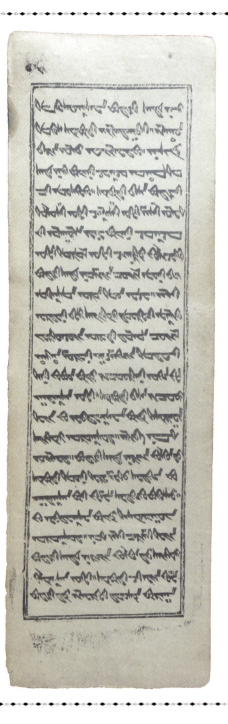

26b

27a

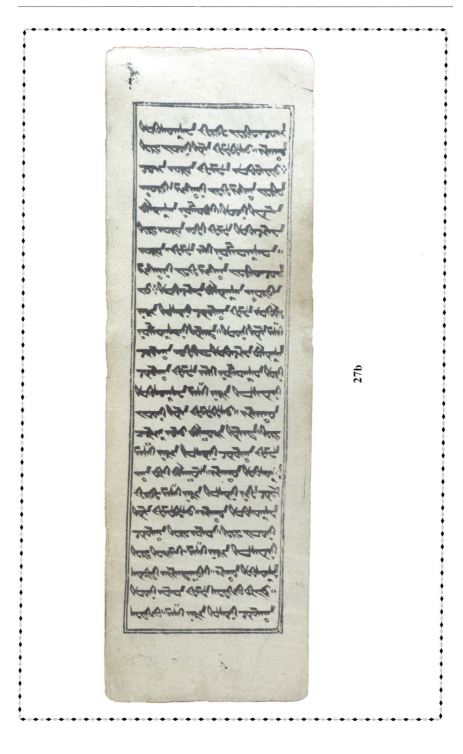

27b

28a

28b

29a

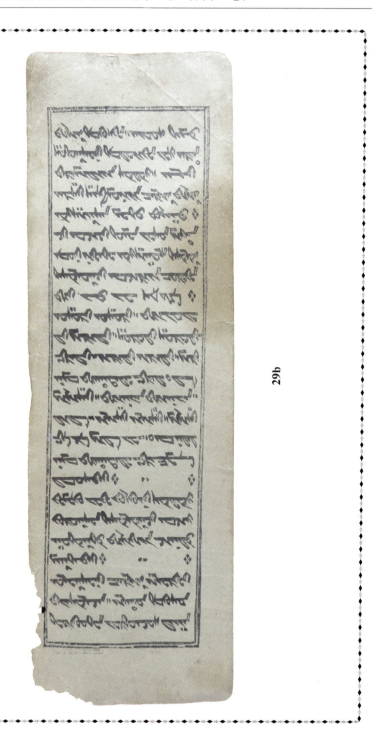

29b

30a

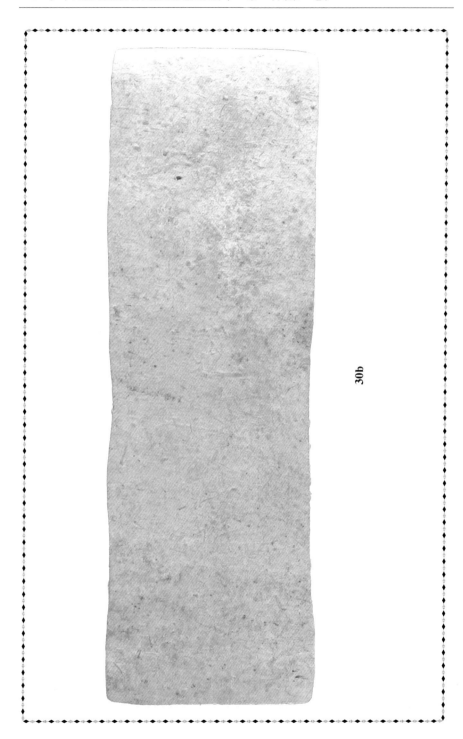

30b

乌莱·普尔白所藏
《能断金刚般若波罗密多经》

　　乌莱·普尔白（1950—　）　新疆维吾尔自治区伊犁哈萨克自治州特克斯县呼吉尔特蒙古乡库热村额鲁特人，牧民。属昭苏六苏木中的阿合苏木人。收藏20余部托忒文古籍文献。

　　《能断金刚般若波罗密多经》（《xutuqtu byiligiyin činadu kürüqsen tasu-laqči očir kemekü yeke külgüni sudur orošiboi》）　17世纪中叶卫拉特高僧咱雅班第达之译经。1795年，在都统特古斯门都之倡议下在伊犁地区木刻，孤本，13×33.4cm，35叶（双面）。

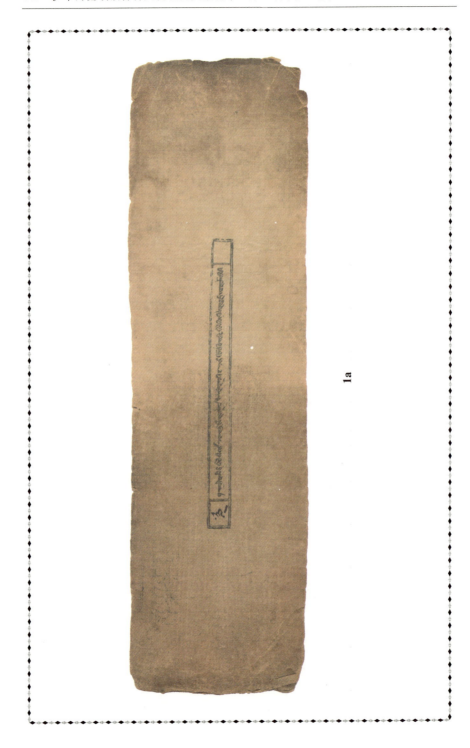

1a

1b

2a

2b

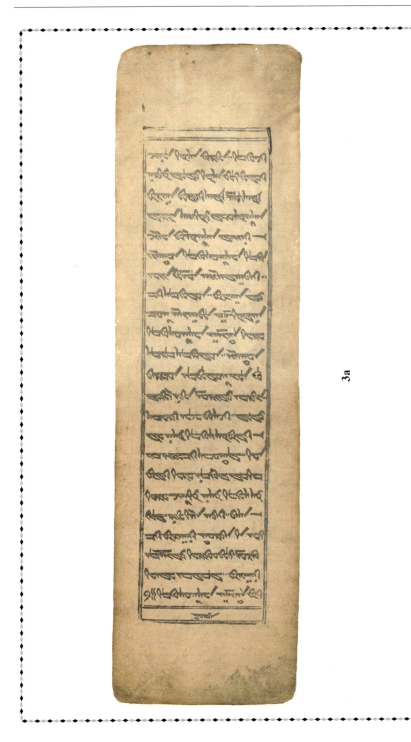

3a

3b

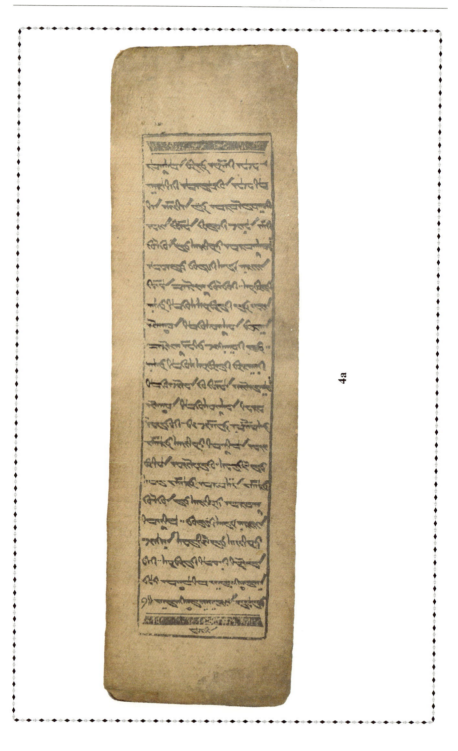

4a

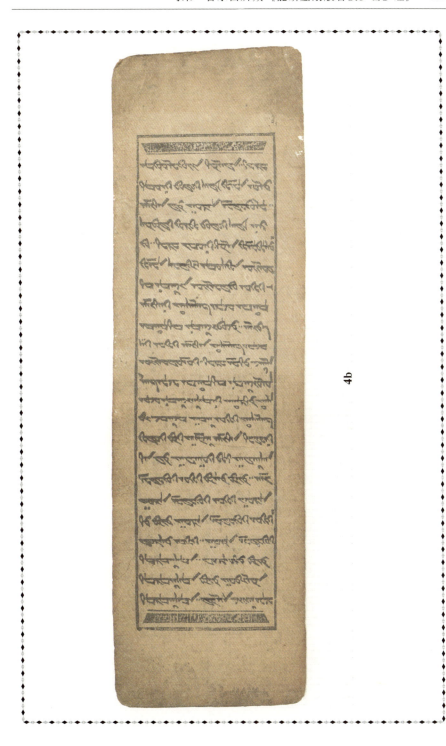

4b

5a

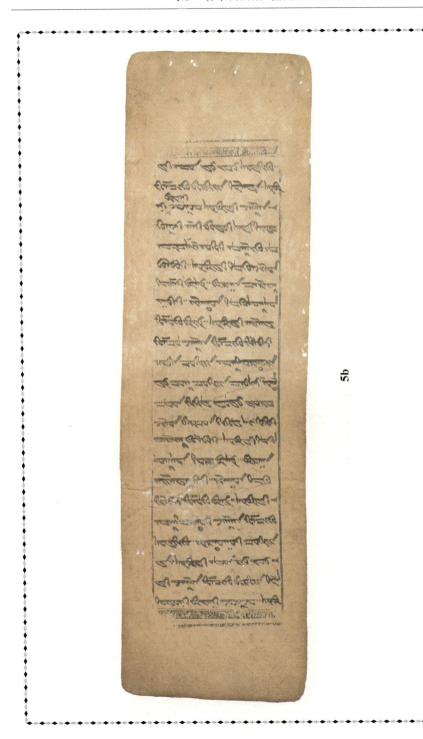

5b

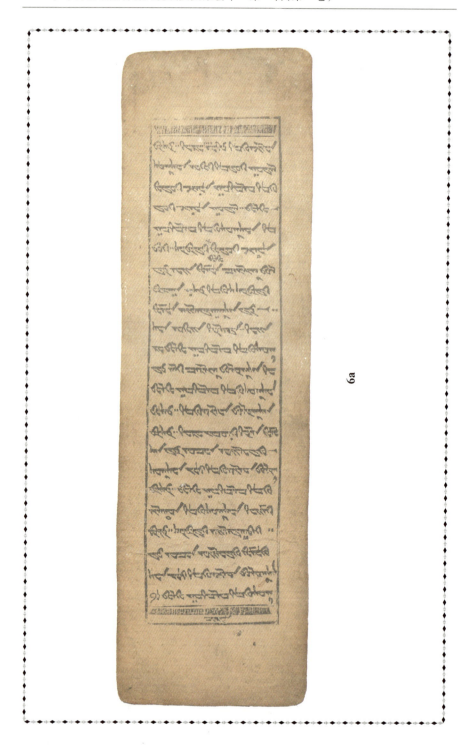

6a

9b

7a

7b

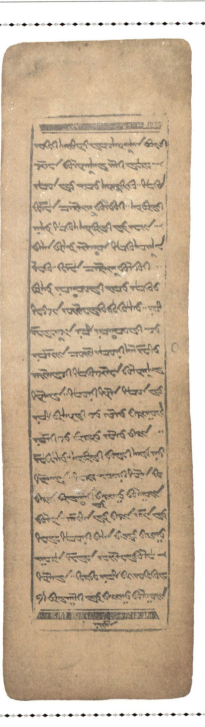

8a

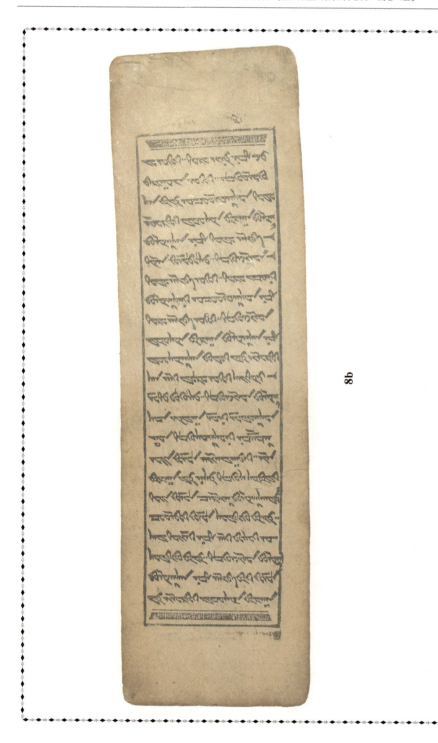

9a

9b

10a

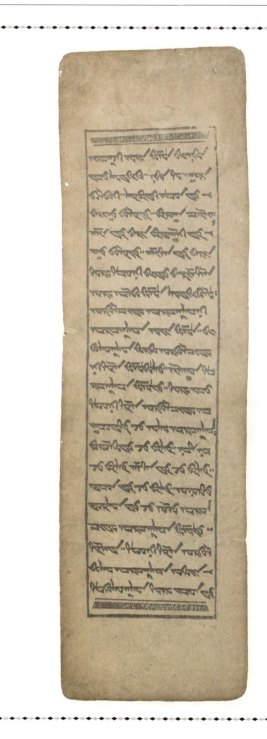

10b

11a

11b

12a

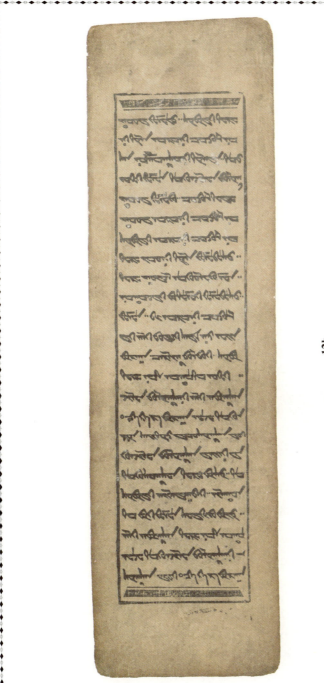

12b

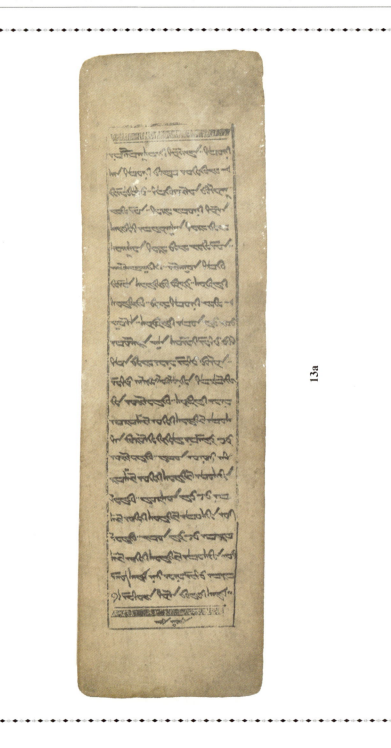

13a

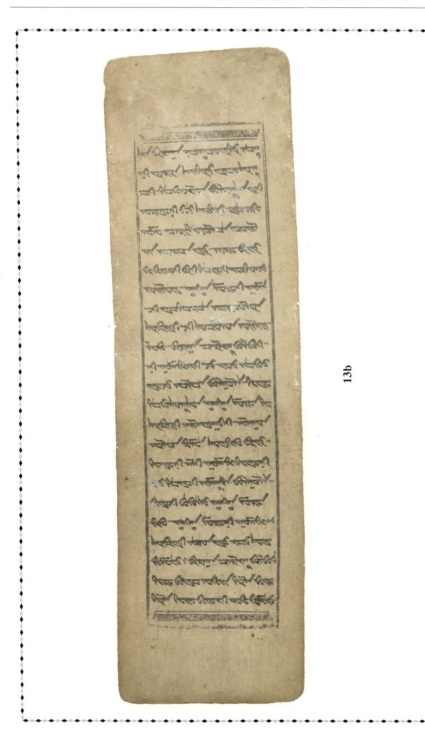

13b

14a

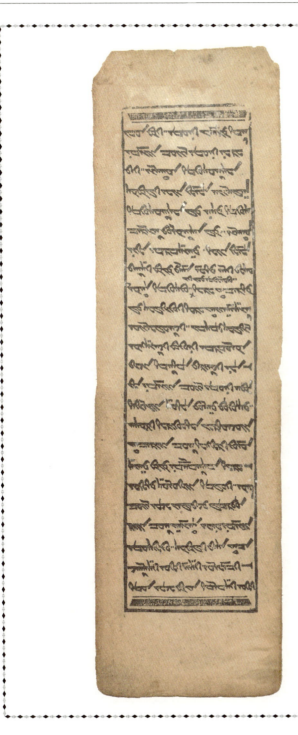

14b

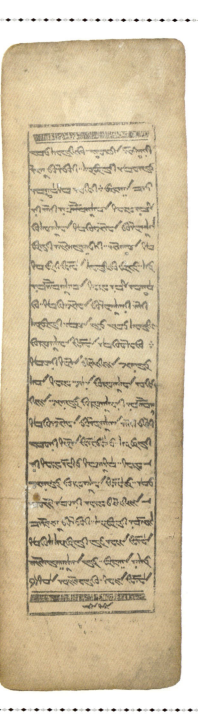

15a

15b

16a

16b

17a

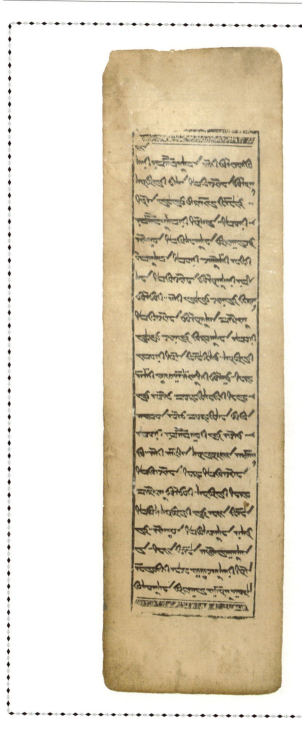

17b

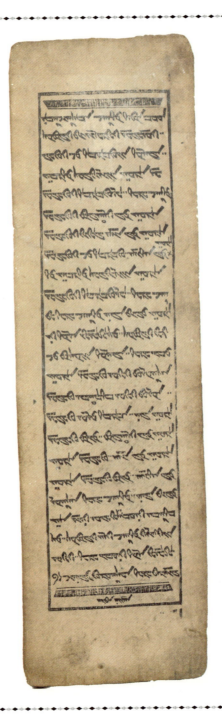

18a

18b

19a

19b

20a

20b

21a

21b

22a

22b

23a

23b

24a

24b

25a

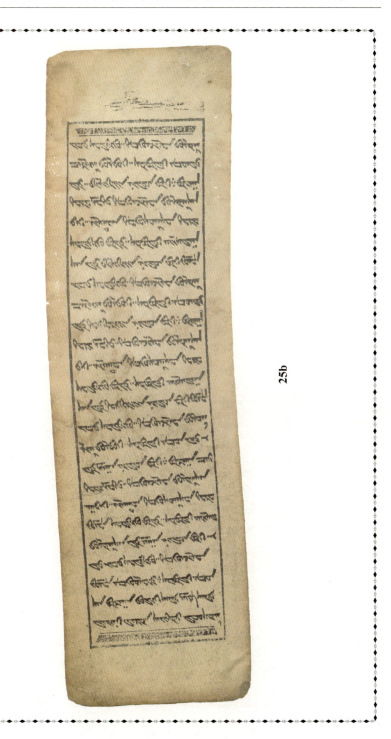

26a

26b

27a

27b

28a

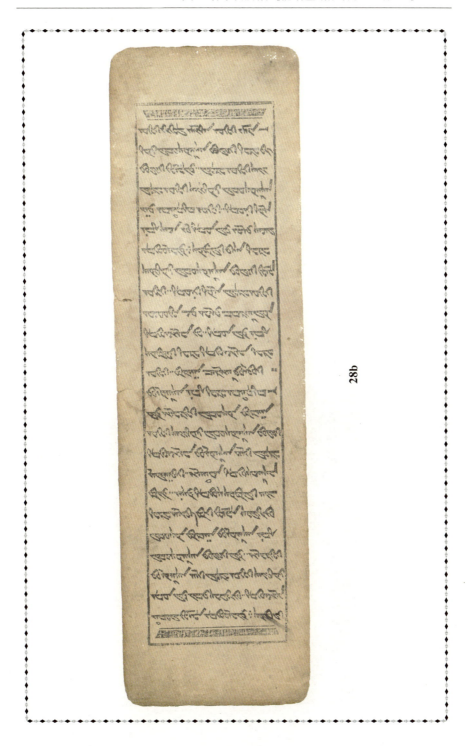

28b

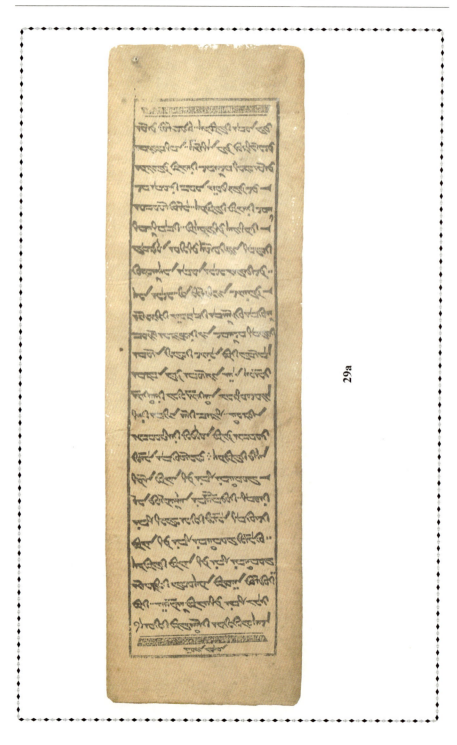

29a

29b

30a

30b

31a

31b

32a

32b

33a

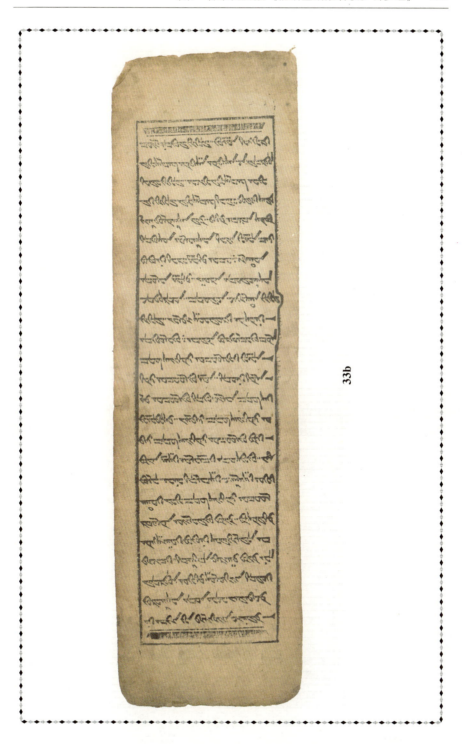

33b

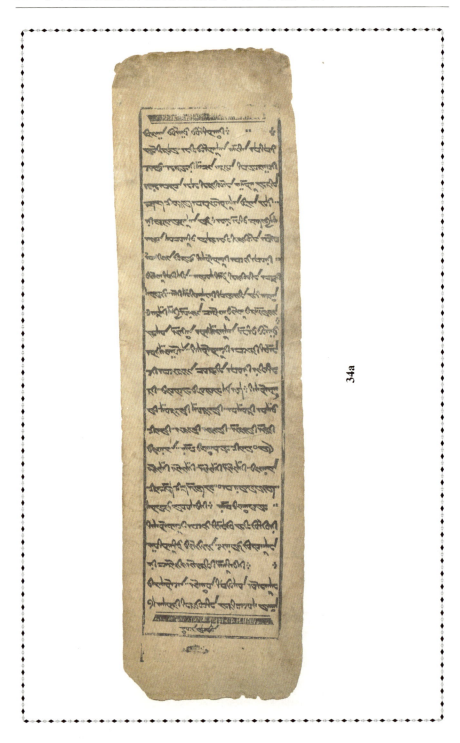

34a

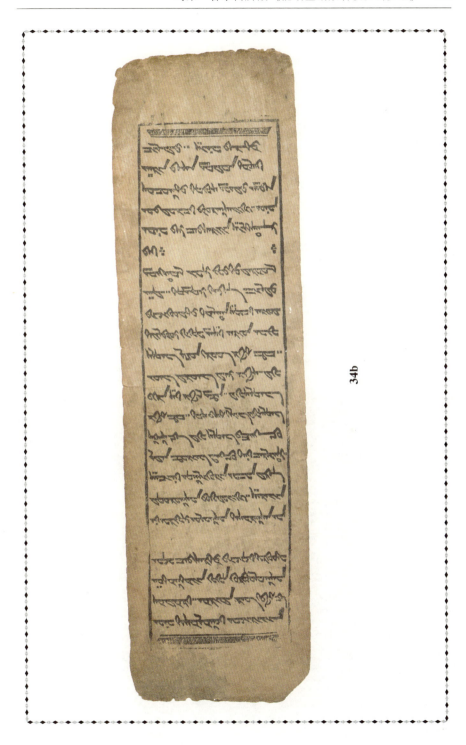

34b

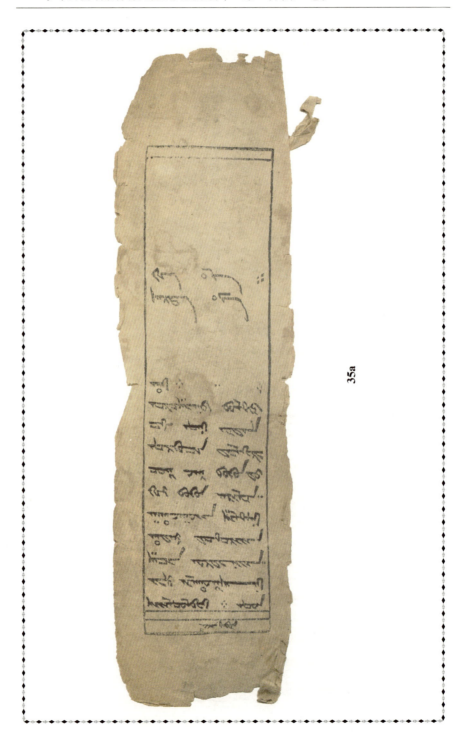

35a

35b

宾巴·苏布赛所藏
《圣者无量寿智大乘经》

宾巴·苏布赛（1951—　）　　新疆维吾尔自治区伊犁哈萨克自治州昭苏县乌尊布拉克乡额鲁特人，退休教师。属昭苏六苏木中的阿合苏木人，乌斯尔额力根。收藏 5 部托忒文古籍文献。

《圣者无量寿智大乘经》（《xutuqtu čaqlaši ügei nasun belge biligtü kemekü yeke külgüni sudur orošibai》）　　17 世纪中叶卫拉特高僧咱雅班第达之译经。清代末期伊犁地区木刻，9×23.4cm，17 叶（双面）。佛教重要典籍。该木刻在伊犁河流域较多见。农四师 76 团一连哈拉·陶克陶夫、昭苏县天山乡德力格尔、昭苏县阿克达拉乡叶尔德尼·夏格加、伊犁种马场朱扎·乌力吉巴图均各藏一部。

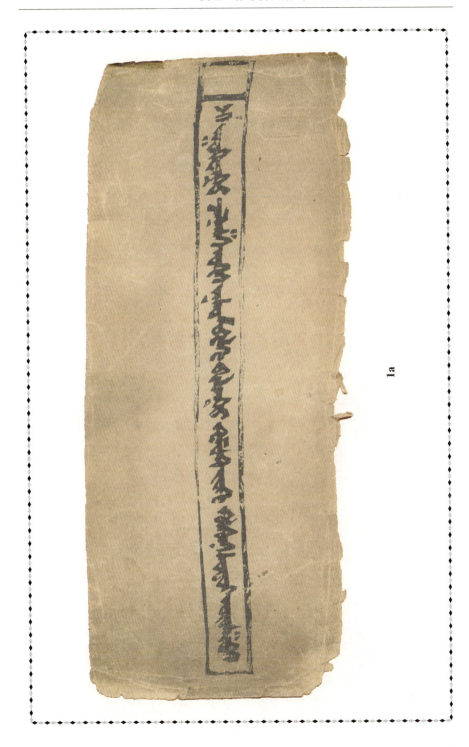

1a

1b

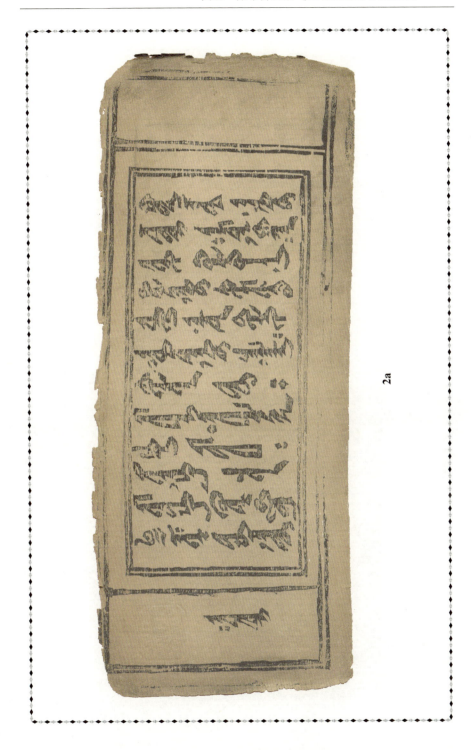

2a

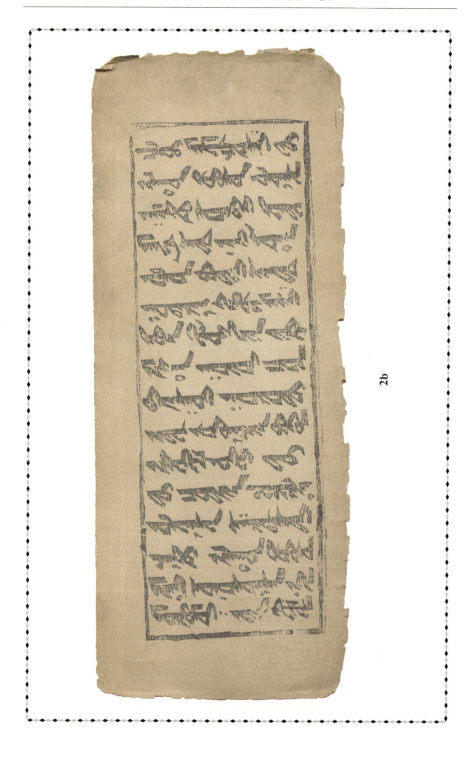

2b

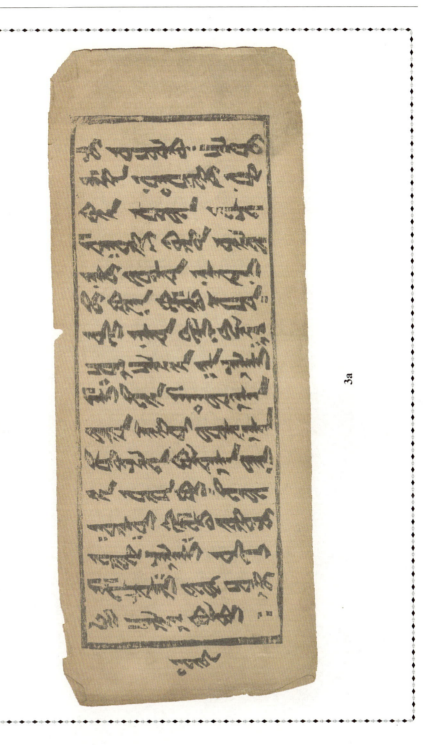

3a

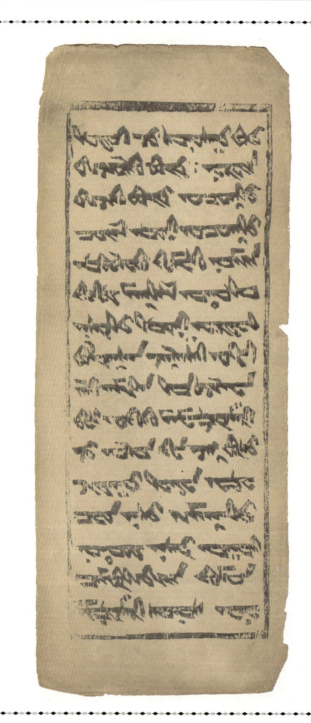

3b

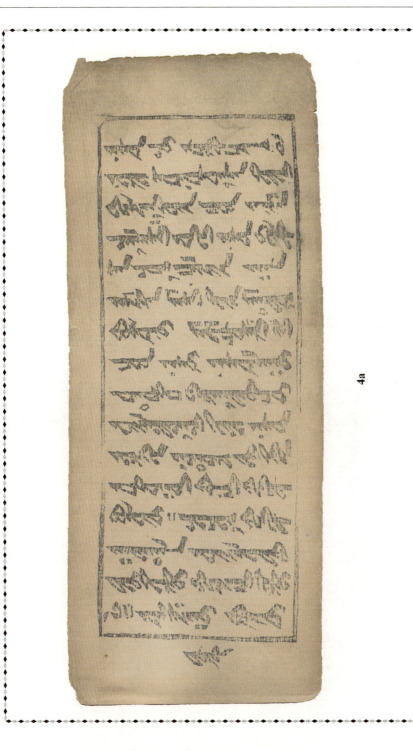

4a

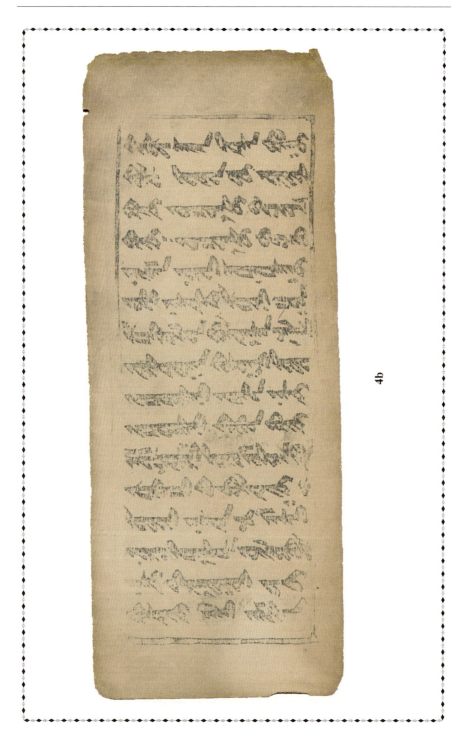

4b

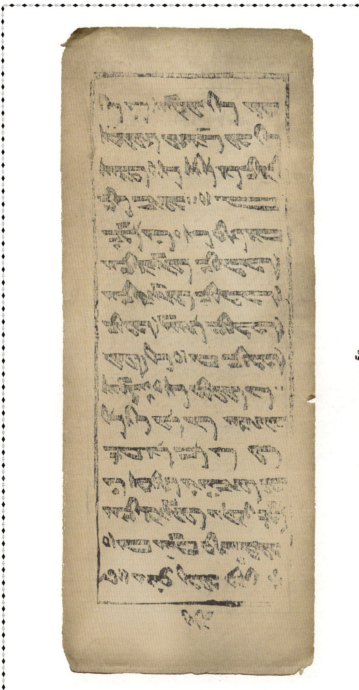

5a

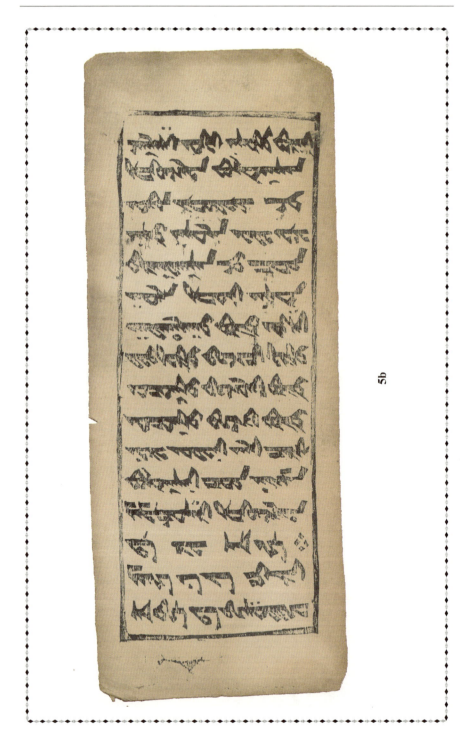

5b

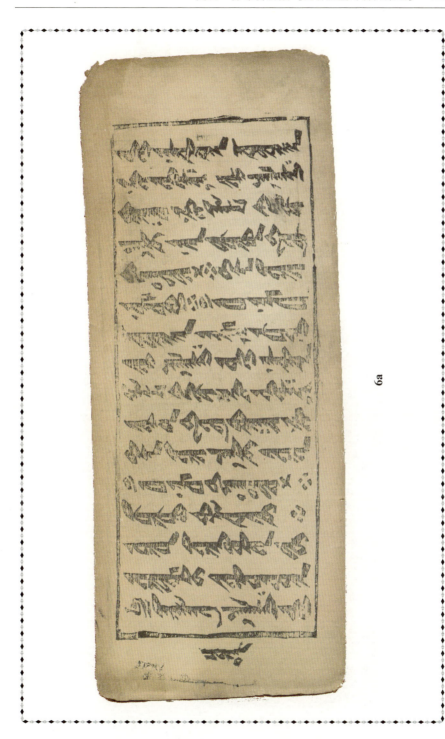

6a

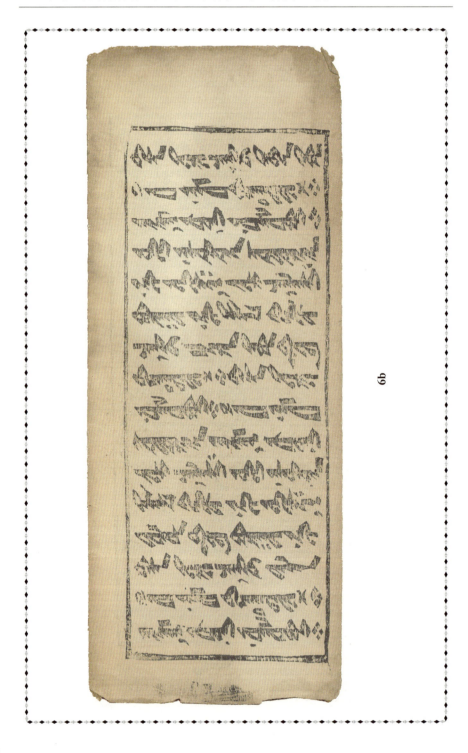

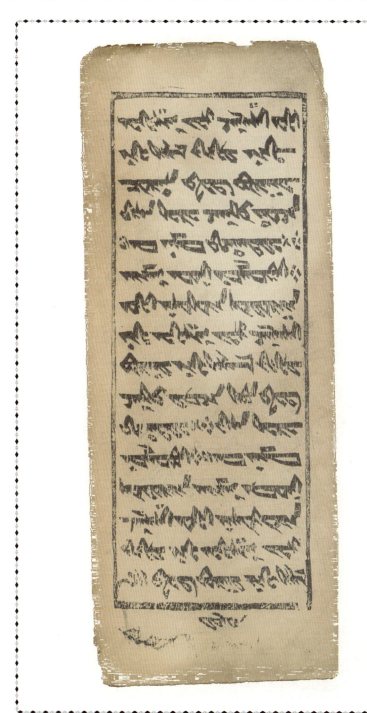

7a

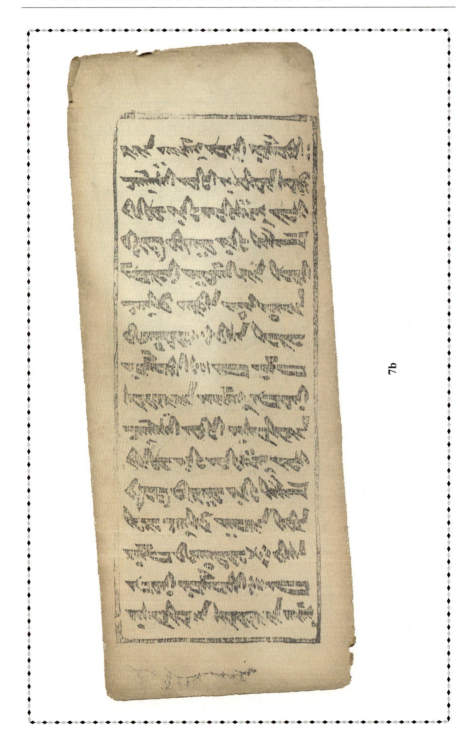

7b

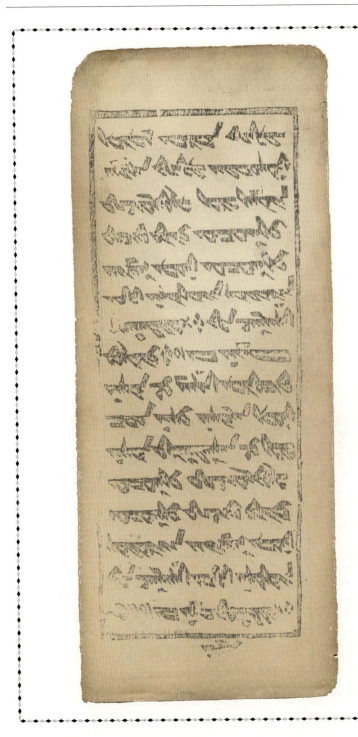

8a

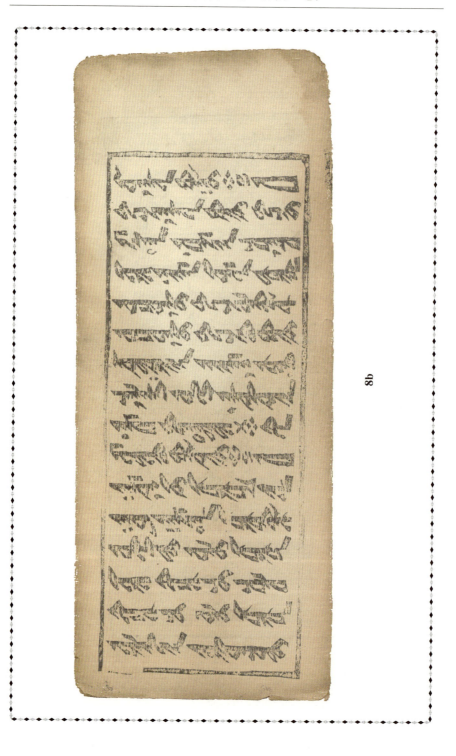

8b

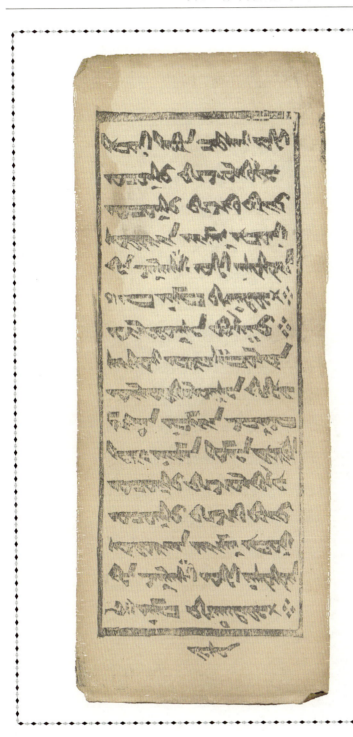

9a

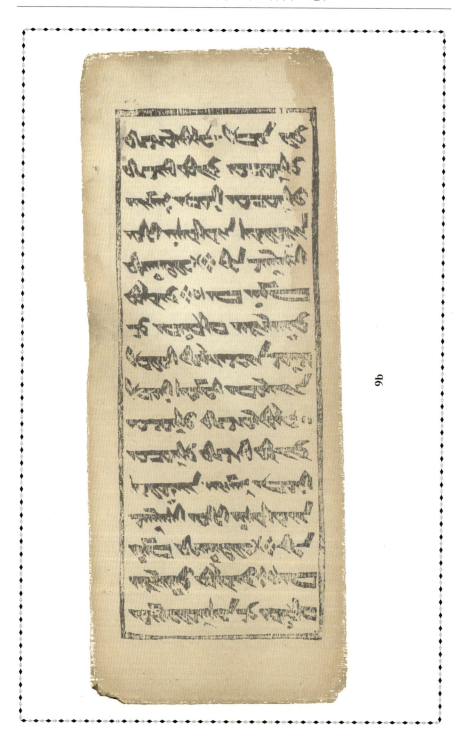

9b

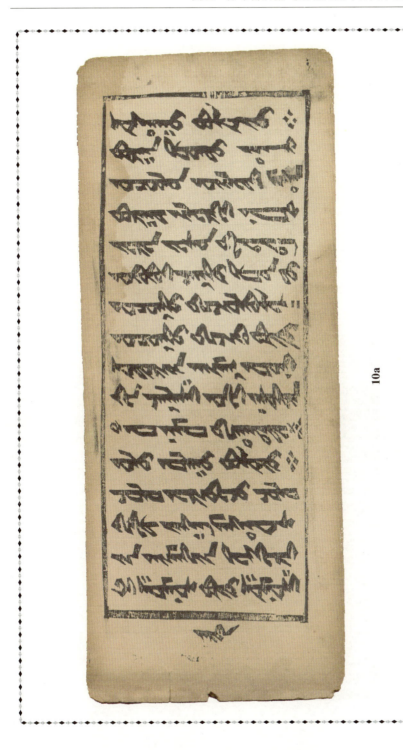

10a

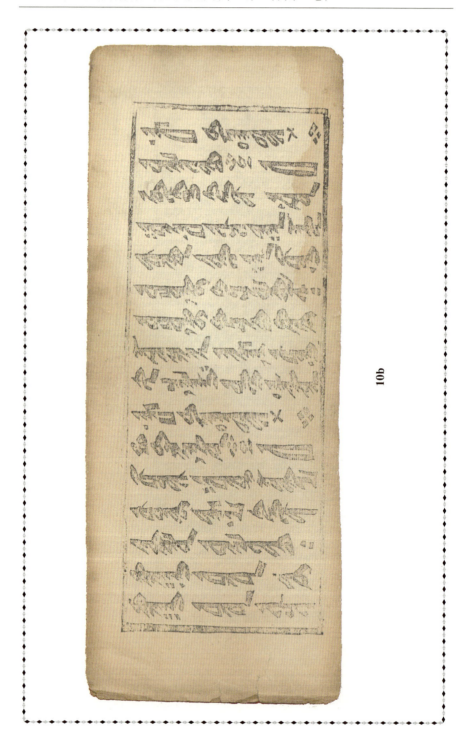

10b

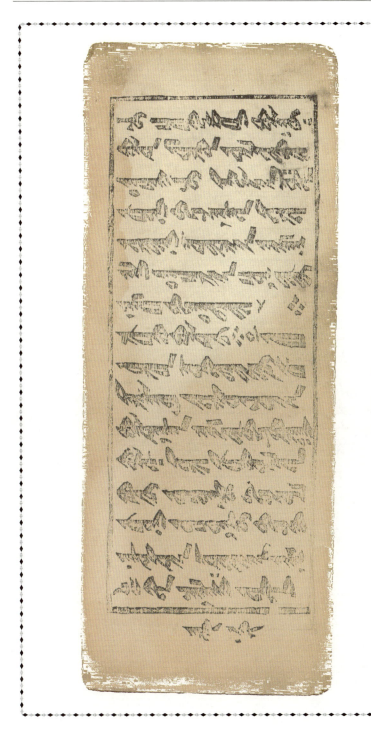

11a

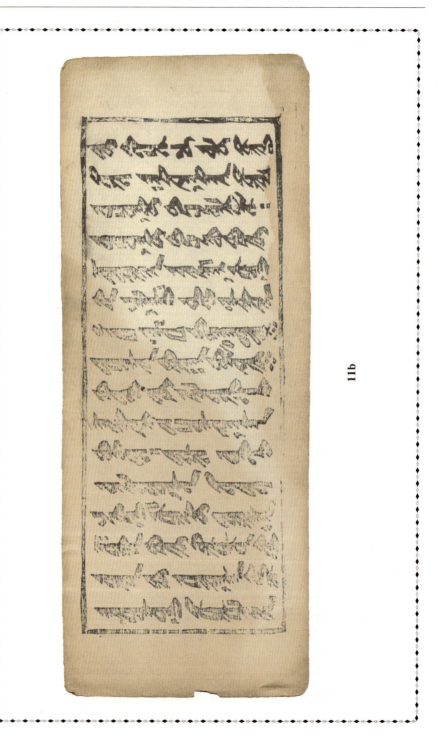

11b

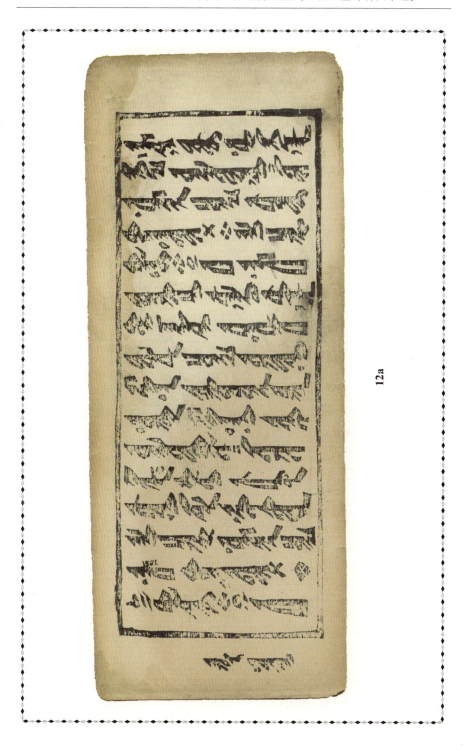

12a

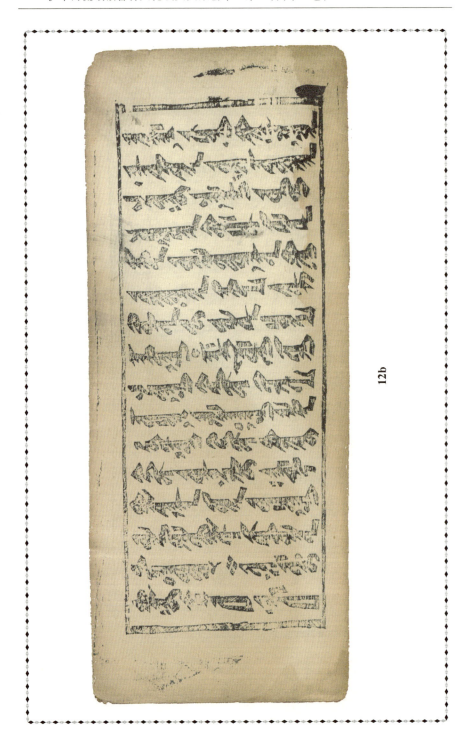

12b

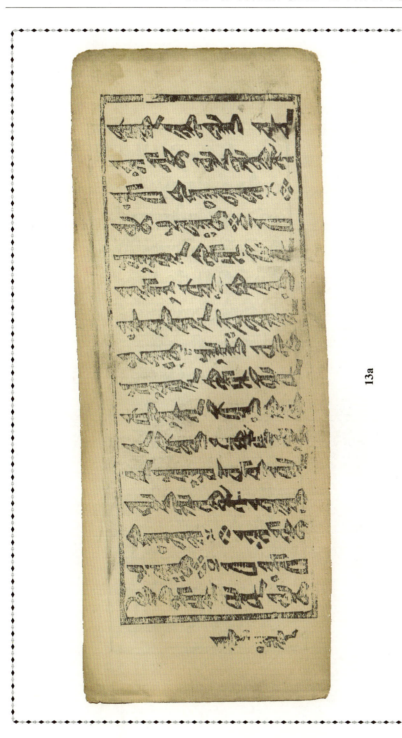

13a

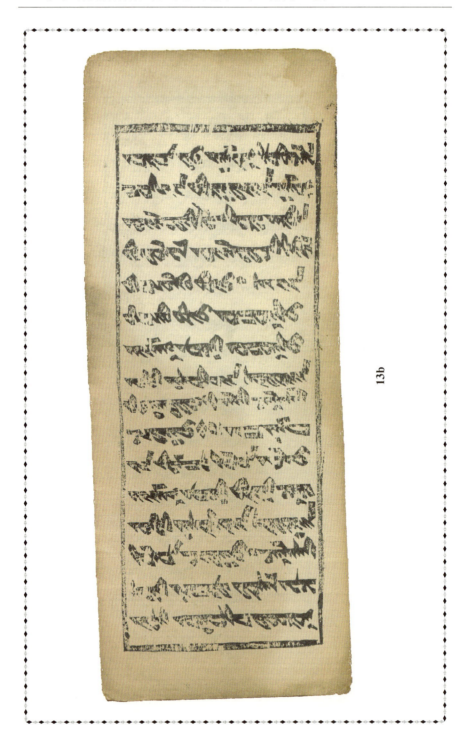

13b

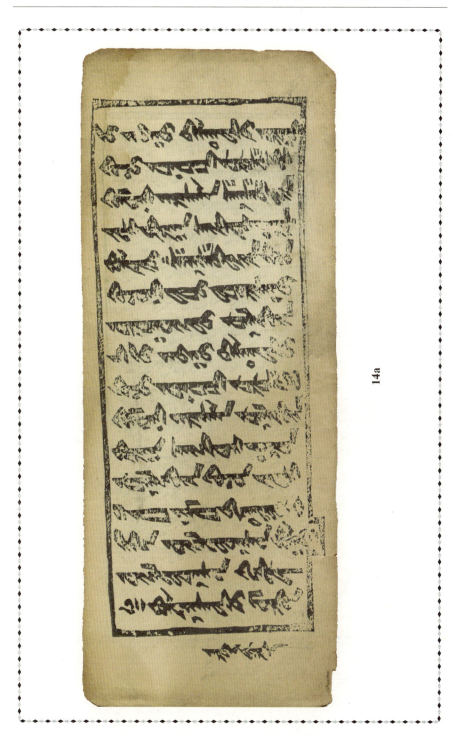

14a

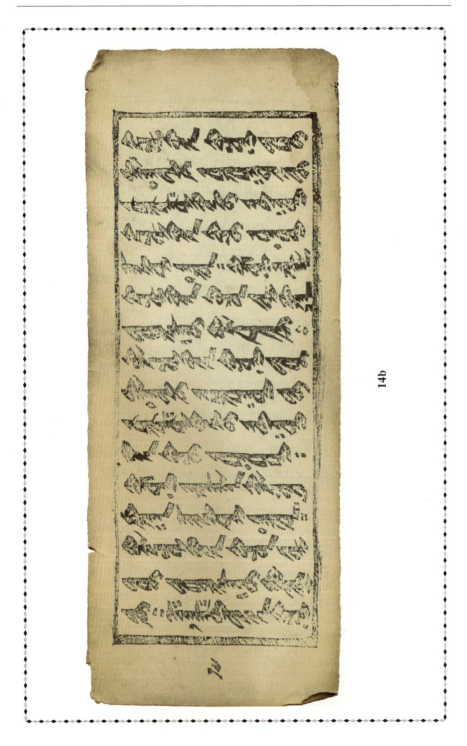

14b

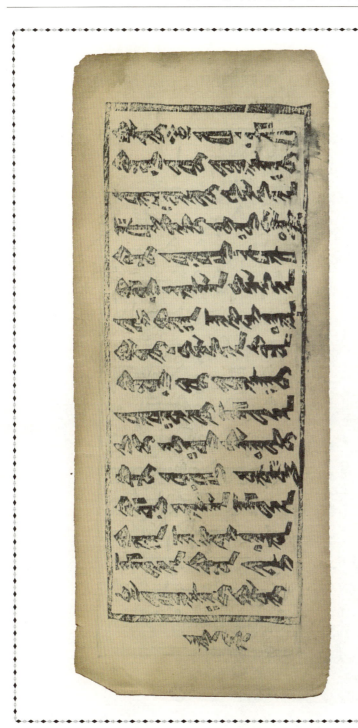

15a

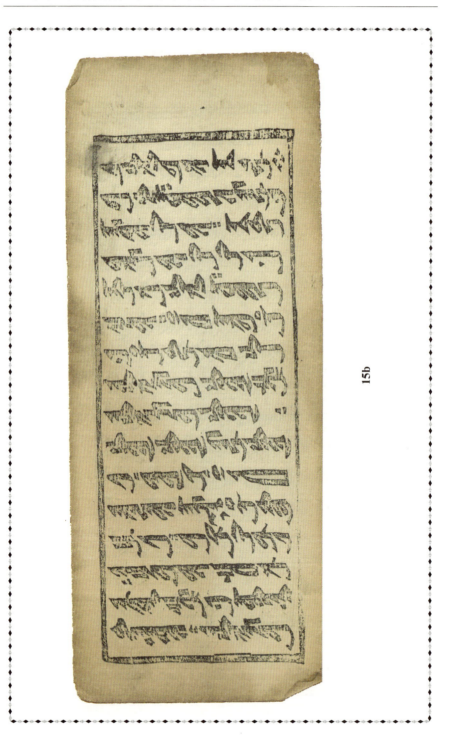

15b

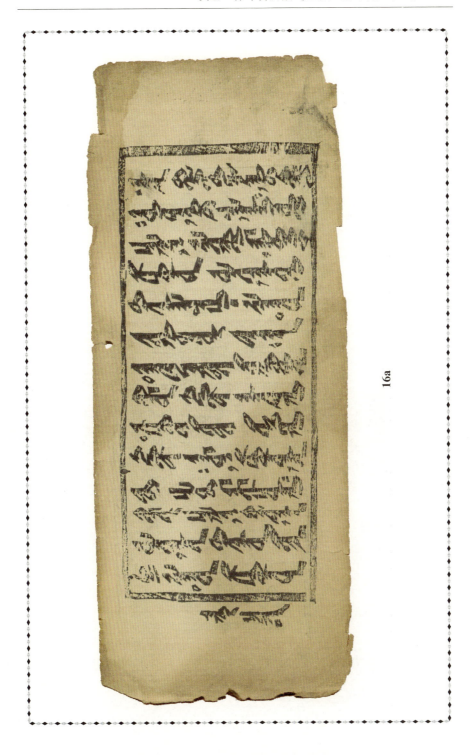

16a

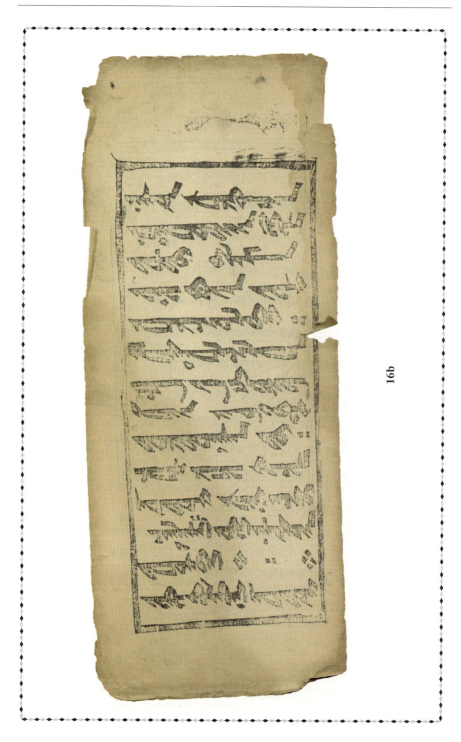

16b

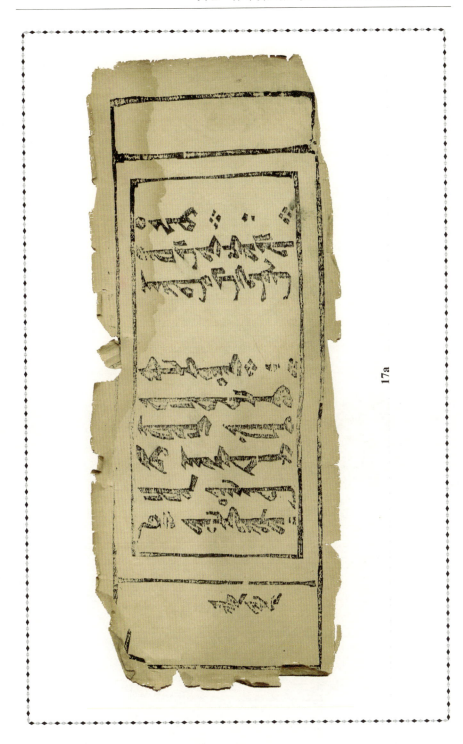

17a

17b

力格希德·浩特勒特古斯所藏
《蒙古溯源史》

力格希德·浩特勒特古斯（1965—2015）　新疆维吾尔自治区伊犁哈萨克自治州伊犁种马场额鲁特人，农民。属昭苏六苏木中的巴苏木人，乌玛特根额力根。收藏30余部托忒文古籍文献。

《蒙古溯源史》（《mongɣoliyin uq ekeyin tuuji》）　唯独伊犁河流域所藏准噶尔编年史，作者是德格台。抄本，线装本，8.8×21cm，14叶（双面）。关于其成书年代学界一直争论不休，是尚未解决的重要问题。

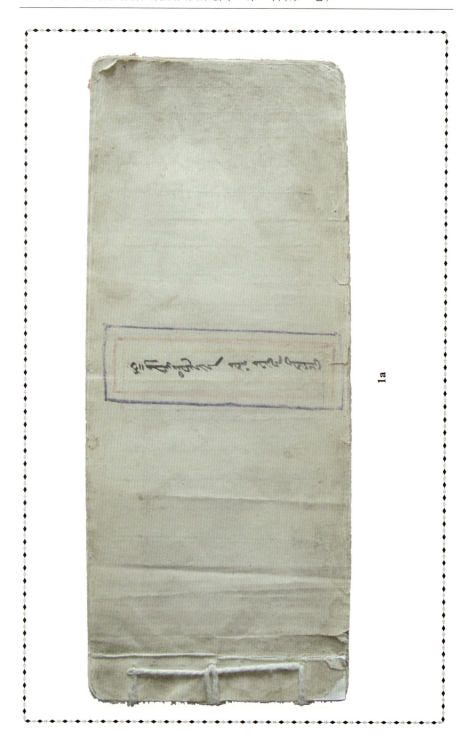

1a

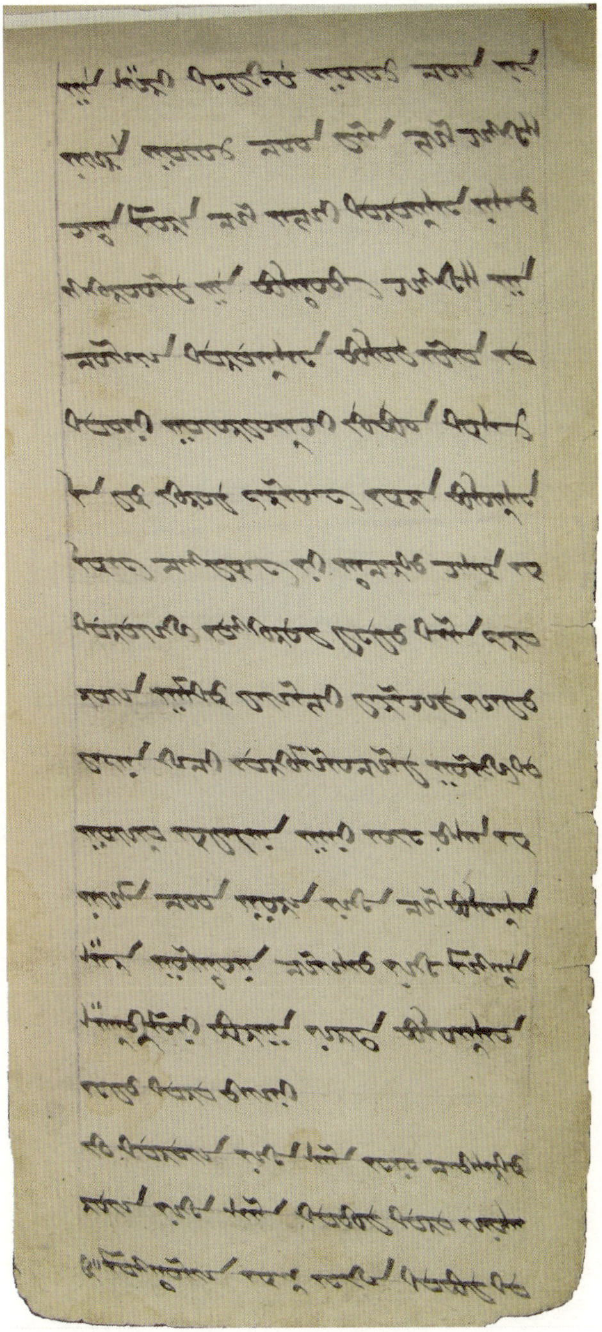

1b

2a

2b

3a

3b

4a

4b

5a

5b

6a

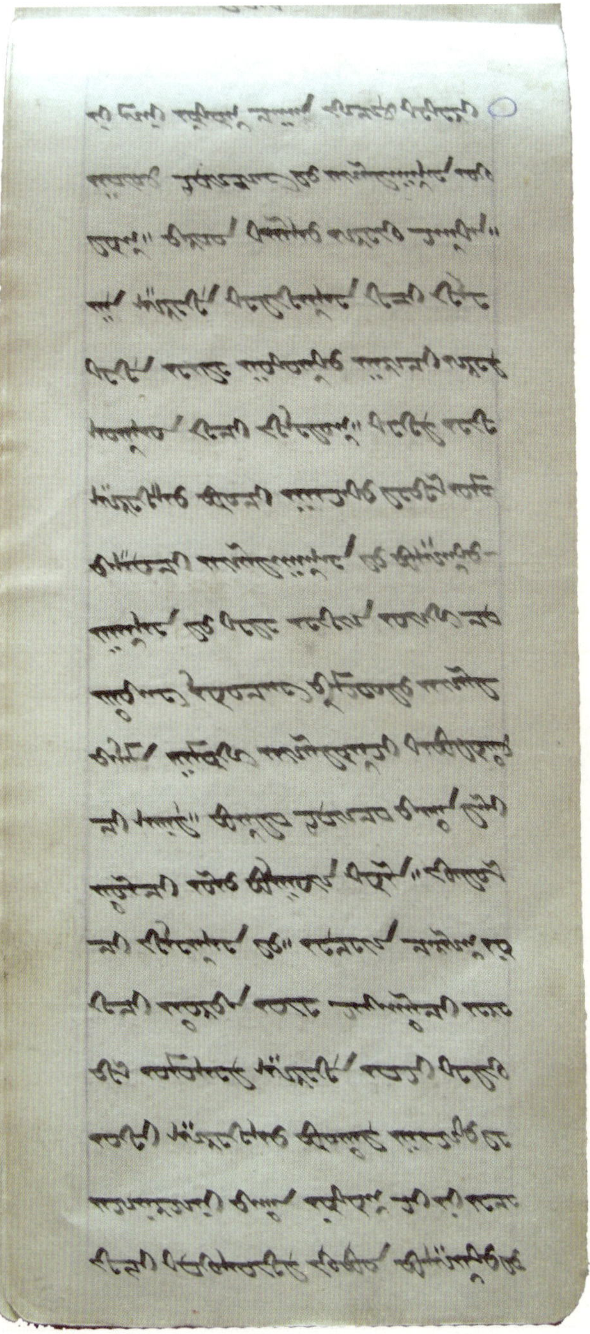

6b

7a

7b

8a

8b

9a

9b

10a

10b

11a

11b

12a

12b

13a

13b

14a

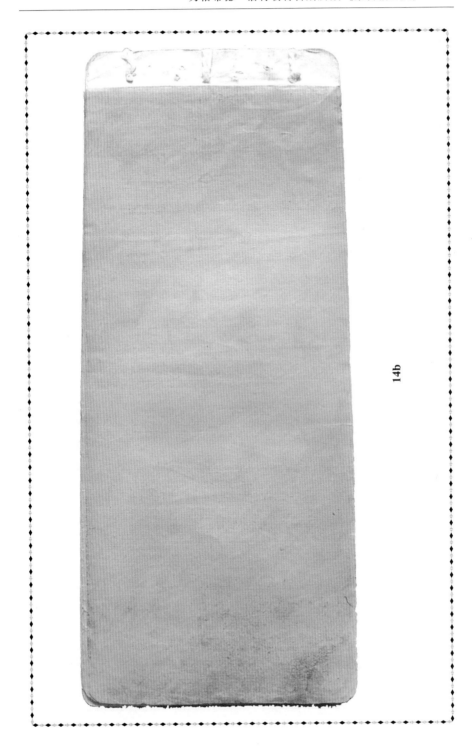

14b

查干·孟和巴图所藏
《准噶尔史——远古的历史》

查干·孟和巴图（1966—　）　新疆维吾尔自治区伊犁哈萨克自治州昭苏县乌尊布拉克乡额鲁特人，医生。属昭苏六苏木中的阿合苏木人，布日德额力根。

《准噶尔史——远古的历史》（《jüün ɣariyin tuuǰi eng urida angxan uridu xoyor orošiboi》）　唯独伊犁河流域所藏准噶尔政教编年史，作者佚名。清代末期抄本，线装本，11×18cm，21叶（双面），结尾部分散失。

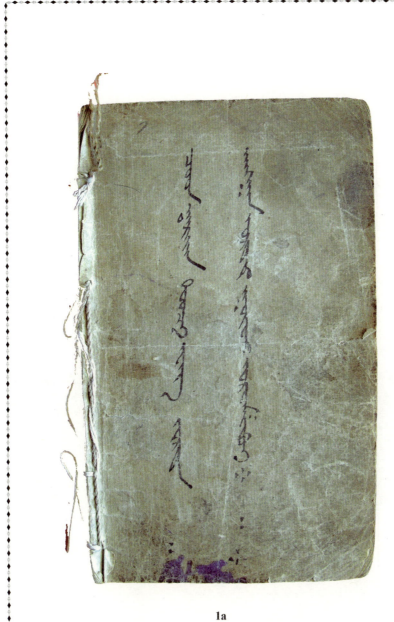

1a

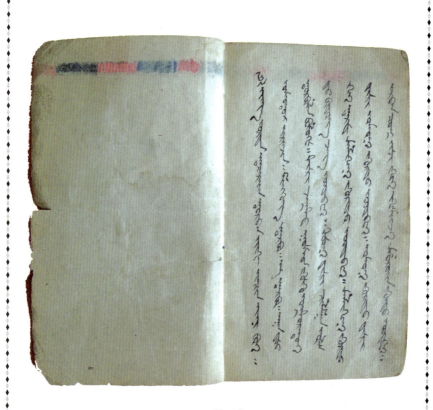

1b—2a

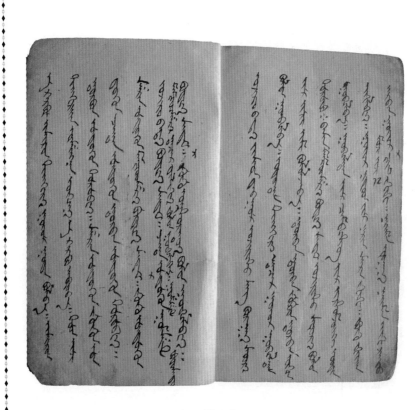

2b—3a

3b—4a

4b—5a

5b—6a

6b—7a

7b—8a

8b—9a

9b—10a

10b—11a

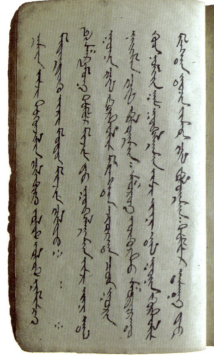

11b—12a

12b—13a

13b—14a

14b—15a

15b—16a

16b—17a

17b—18a

18b—19a

19b—20a

20b—21a

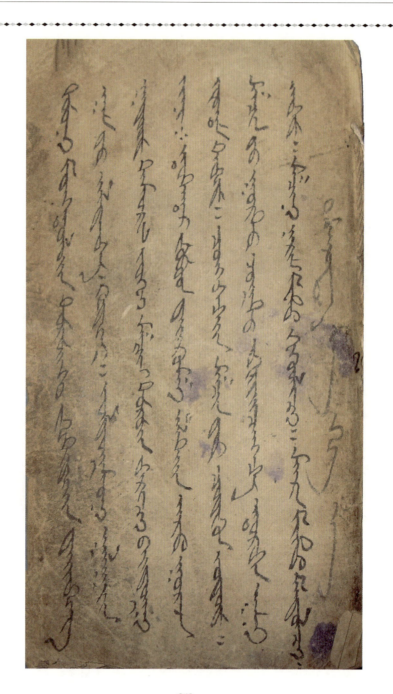

21b

图书在版编目（CIP）数据

伊犁河流域额鲁特人托忒文文献荟萃 . 第一辑：全三卷：蒙古语 /
叶尔达主编 . —北京：中国社会科学出版社，2016.10
　（大国学研究文库）
　ISBN 978 - 7 - 5161 - 8496 - 7

　Ⅰ. ①伊…　Ⅱ. ①叶…　Ⅲ. ①厄鲁特—古籍—汇编—中国—蒙古语
（中国少数民族语言）　Ⅳ. ①K289

中国版本图书馆 CIP 数据核字（2016）第 156686 号

出 版 人	赵剑英
责任编辑	史慕鸿
责任校对	李四新
责任印制	戴 宽

出　　　版	中国社会科学出版社
社　　　址	北京鼓楼西大街甲 158 号
邮　　　编	100720
网　　　址	http://www.csspw.cn
发 行 部	010 - 84083685
门 市 部	010 - 84029450
经　　　销	新华书店及其他书店

印刷装订	北京君升印刷有限公司
版　　　次	2016 年 10 月第 1 版
印　　　次	2016 年 10 月第 1 次印刷

开　　　本	710 × 1000　1/16
印　　　张	58.25
字　　　数	508 千字
定　　　价	298.00 元（全三卷）

第二卷目录

第 二 卷

敖其尔·敖仑巴雅尔所藏
《五守护神大乘经》

敖其尔·敖仑巴雅尔（1957— ） 新疆维吾尔自治区伊犁哈萨克自治州昭苏县洪纳海乡喀拉苏村额鲁特人，农民。属昭苏六苏木中的阿合苏木人，门德额力根。

《五守护神大乘经》（《banzaraqča》） 佛教重要典籍之一，由《说大千摧破佛母心藏陀罗尼》、《大寒林经》等五部经书组成。清代抄本，14×50cm，五部经书分别有 34、40、27、15、10 叶（双面），有佛像图，破损严重，收藏者以黄、蓝、绿、白纸来全面修复。

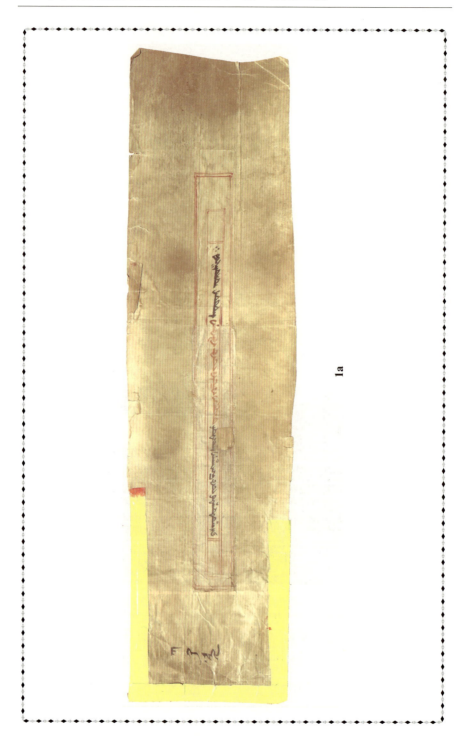

1a

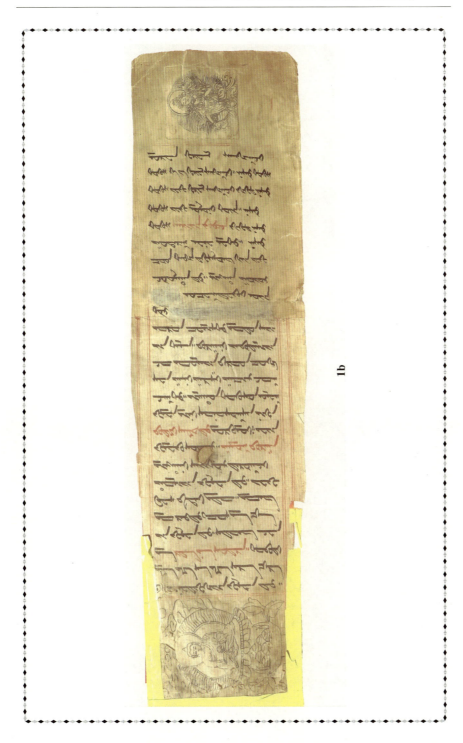

1b

2a

2b

3a

3b

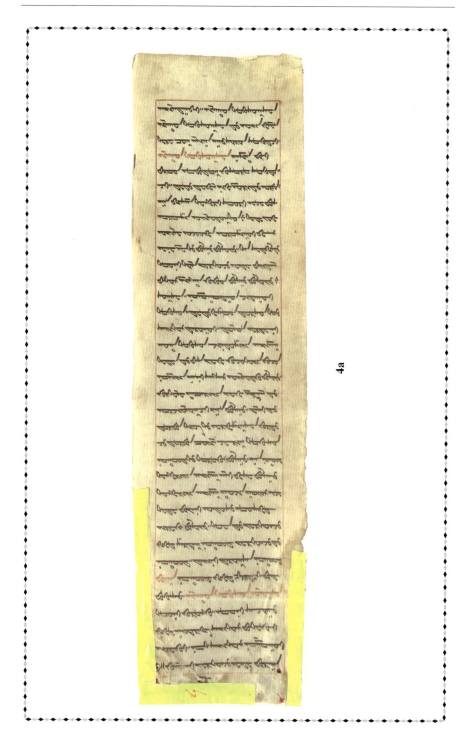

4a

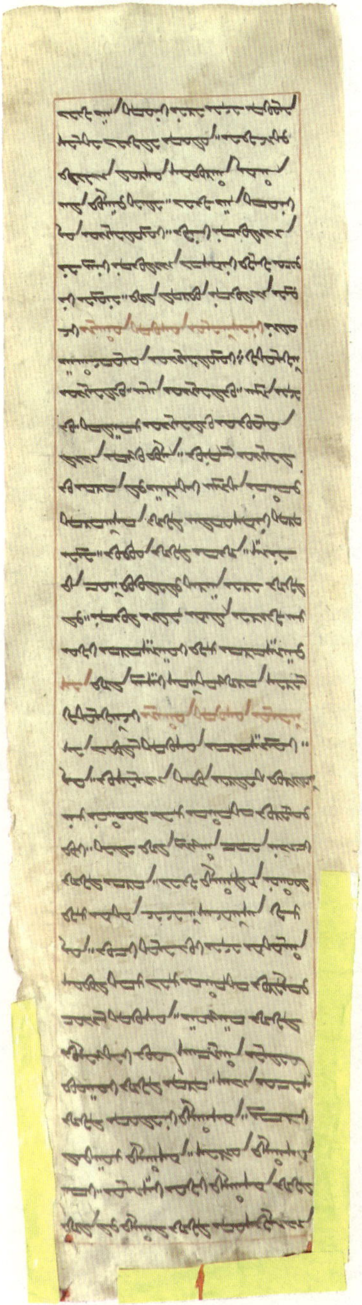

4b

5a

5b

6a

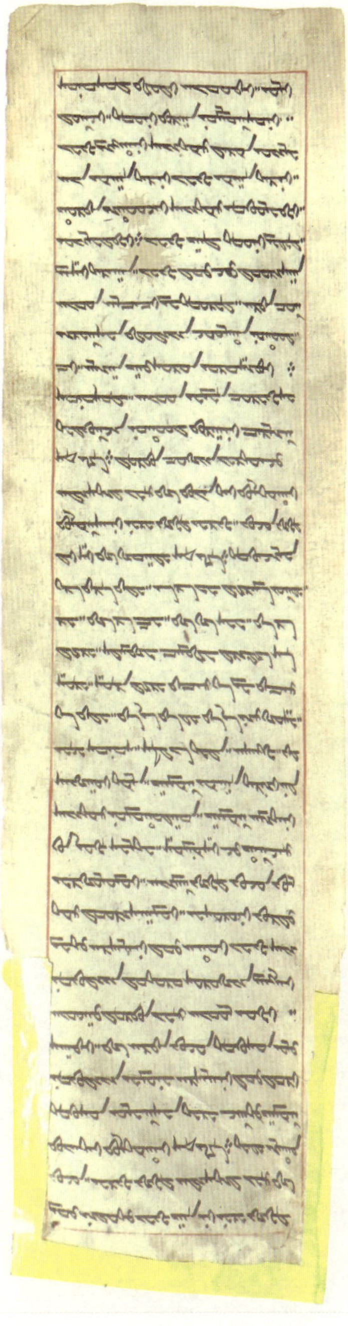

6b

7a

7b

8a

8b

9a

9b

10a

10b

11a

11b

12a

12b

13a

13b

14a

14b

15a

15b

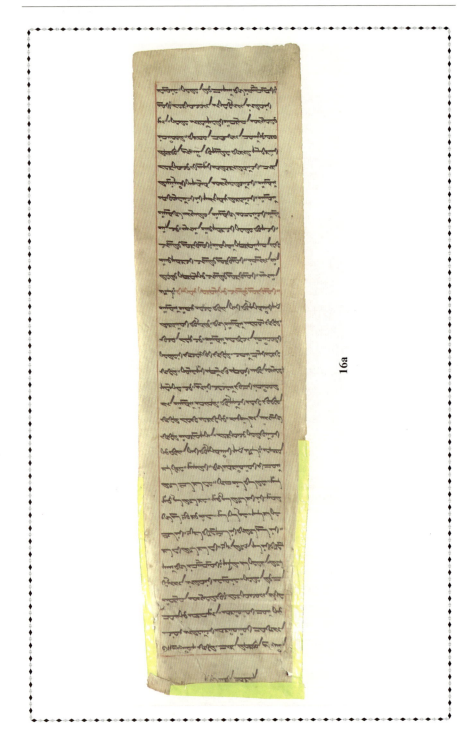

16a

16b

17a

17b

18a

18b

19a

19b

20a

20b

21a

21b

22a

22b

23a

23b

24a

24b

25a

25b

26a

26b

27a

27b

28a

28b

29a

29b

30a

30b

31a

31b

32a

32b

33a

33b

34a

34b

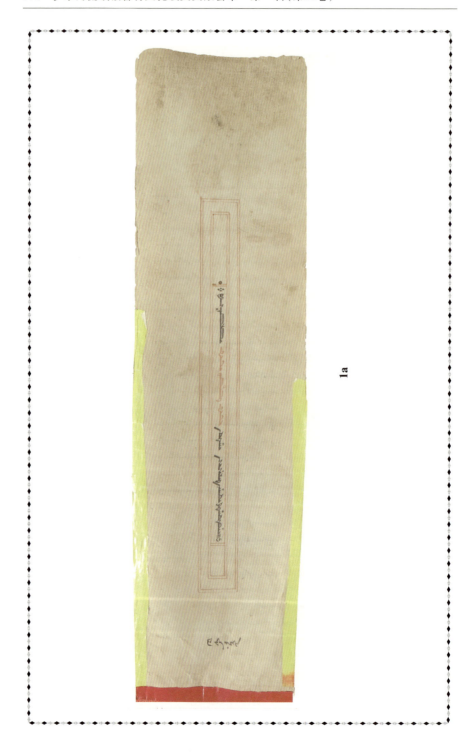

1a

1b

2a

2b

3a

3b

4a

4b

5a

5b

6a

66

7a

7b

8a

8b

9a

9b

10a

10b

11a

11b

12a

12b

13a

13b

14a

14b

15a

15b

16a

16b

17a

17b

18a

18b

19a

19b

20a

20b

21a

21b

22a

22b

23a

23b

24a

24b

25a

25b

26a

26b

27a

27b

28a

28b

29a

29b

30a

30b

31a

31b

32a

32b

33a

33b

34a

34b

35a

35b

36a

36b

37a

37b

38a

38b

39a

39b

40a

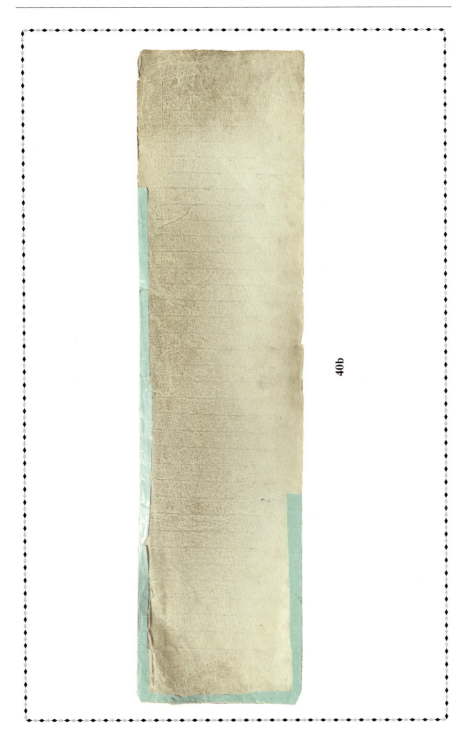

40b

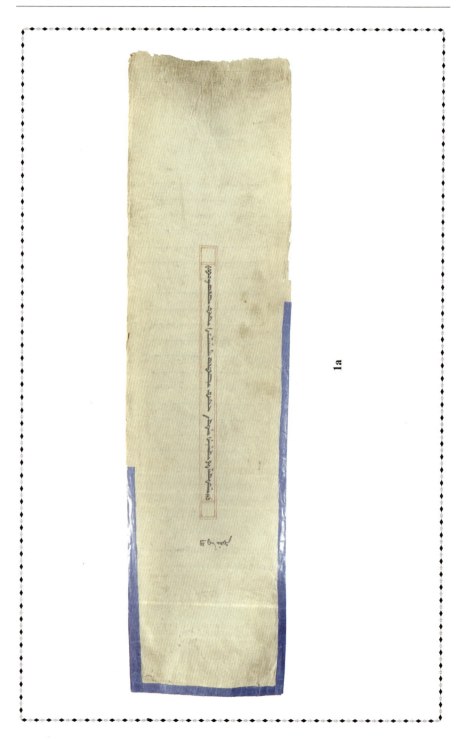

1a

1b

2a

2b

3a

3b

4a

4b

5a

5b

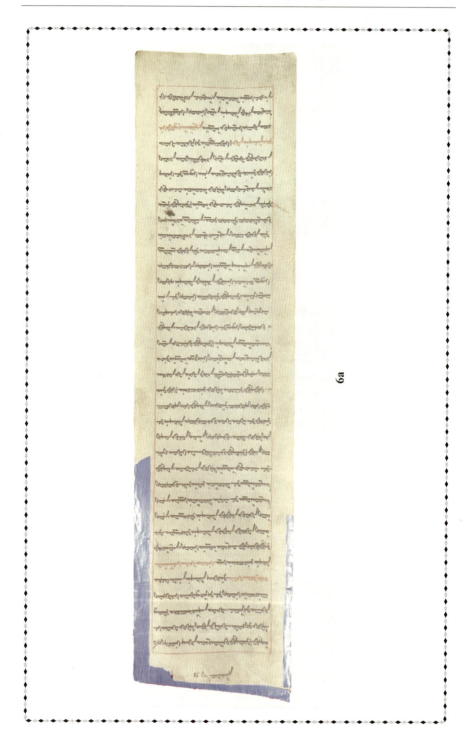

6a

6b

7a

7b

8a

8b

9a

9b

10a

10b

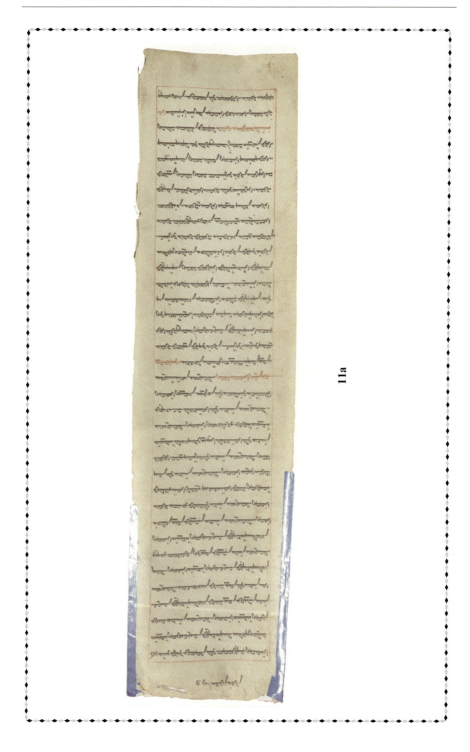

11a

11b

12a

12b

13a

13b

14a

14b

15a

15b

16a

16b

17a

17b

18a

18b

19a

19b

20a

20b

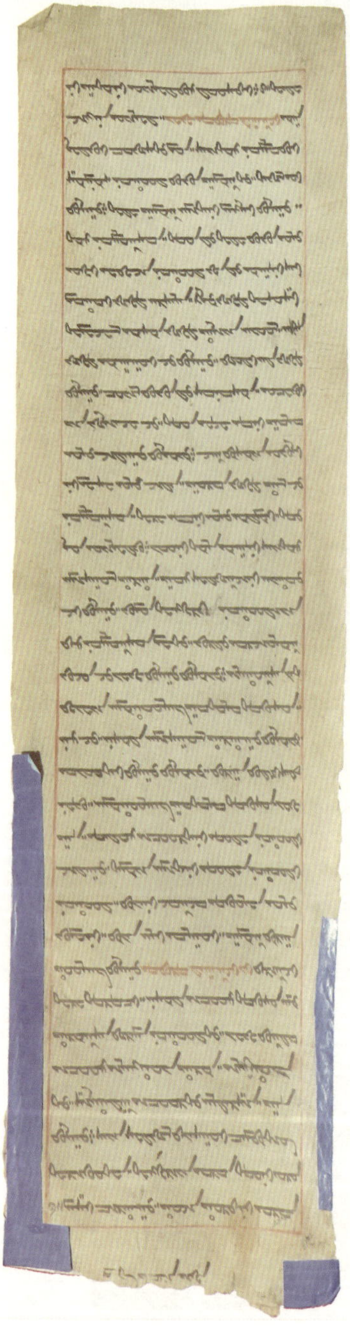

21a

21b

22a

22b

23a

23b

24a

24b

25a

25b

26a

26b

27a

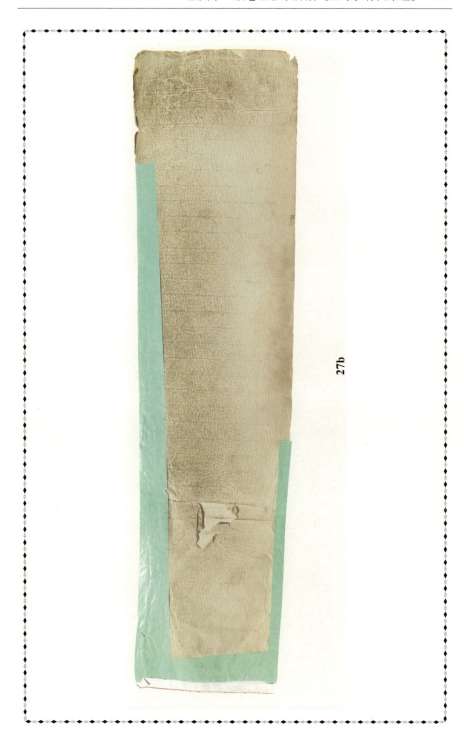

27b

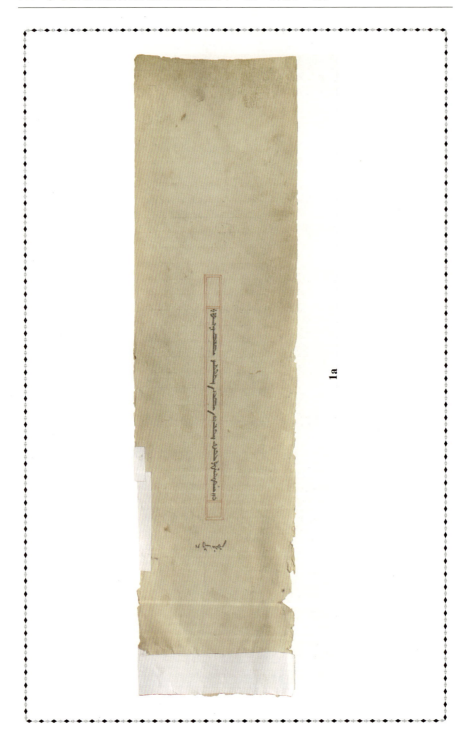

1a

2a

2b

3a

3b

4a

4b

5a

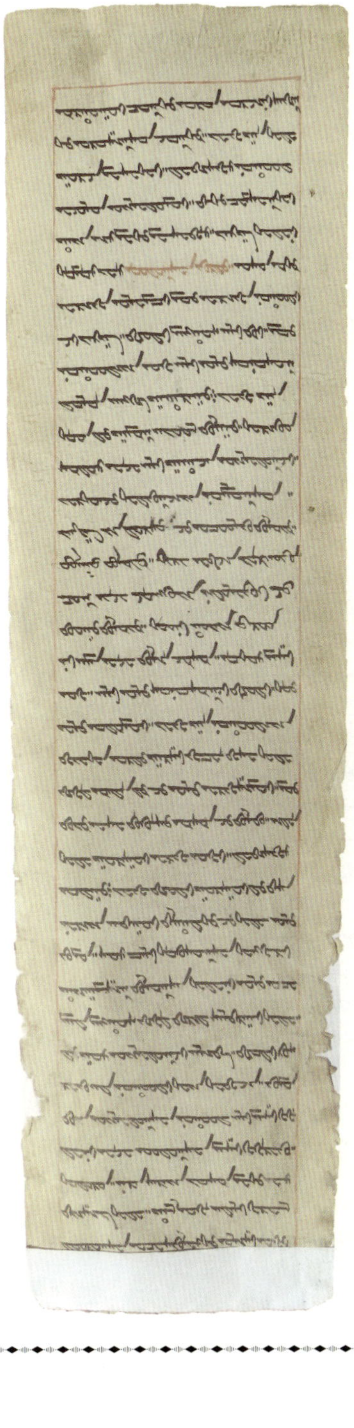

5b

6a

6b

7a

7b

8a

8b

9a

9b

10a

10b

11a

11b

12a

12b

13a

13b

14a

14b

15a

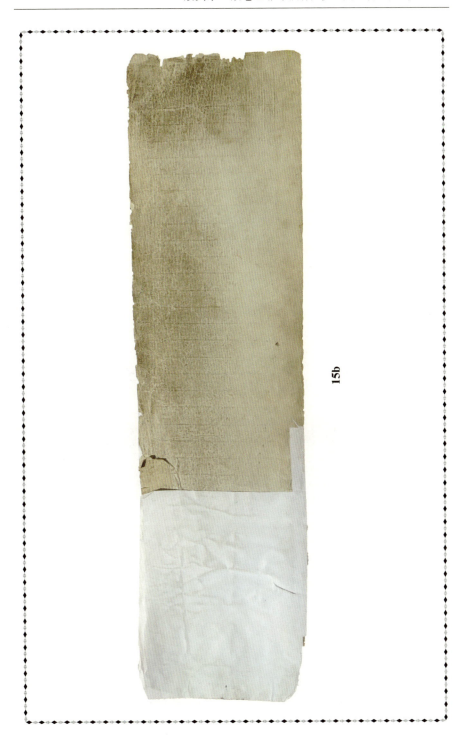

15b

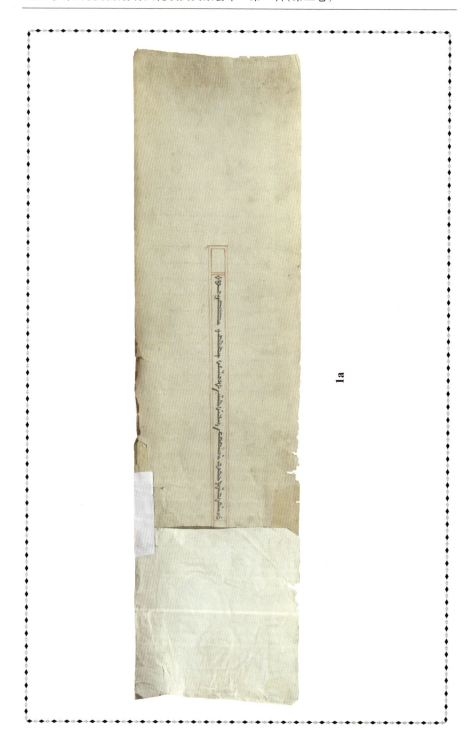

1a

1b

2a

2b

3a

3b

4a

4b

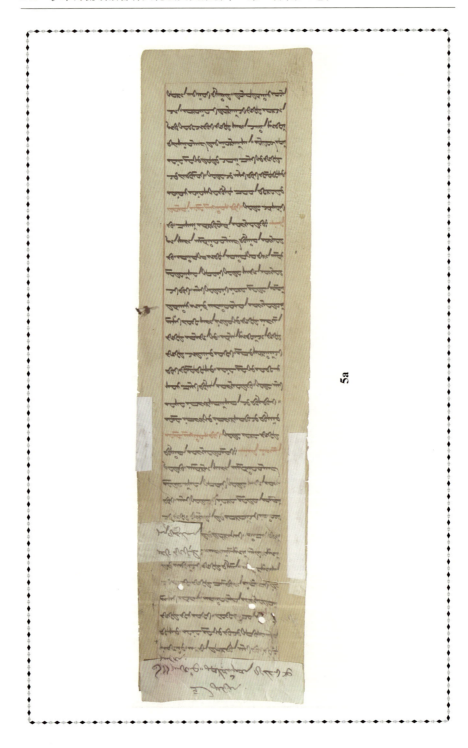

5a

5b

6a

6b

7a

7b

8a

8b

9a

9b

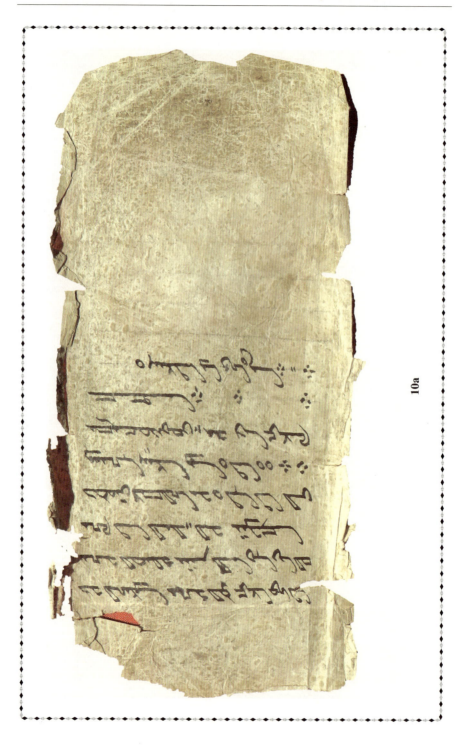

10a

10b

巴图图布欣·宾巴所藏
《绿度母传》

    巴图图布欣·宾巴（1971—　）　新疆维吾尔自治区伊犁哈萨克自治州昭苏县昭苏镇额鲁特人，个体户。属昭苏六苏木中的拿苏木人，奥日斯额力根，诵经者——哈拉巴嘎希。

    《绿度母传》（《baɣma ekeyin tuuǰi orošiboi ara baluu》）　托忒文重要文学作品。成书年代不详，佚名。清代抄本，10.5×30.5cm，17 叶（双面）。

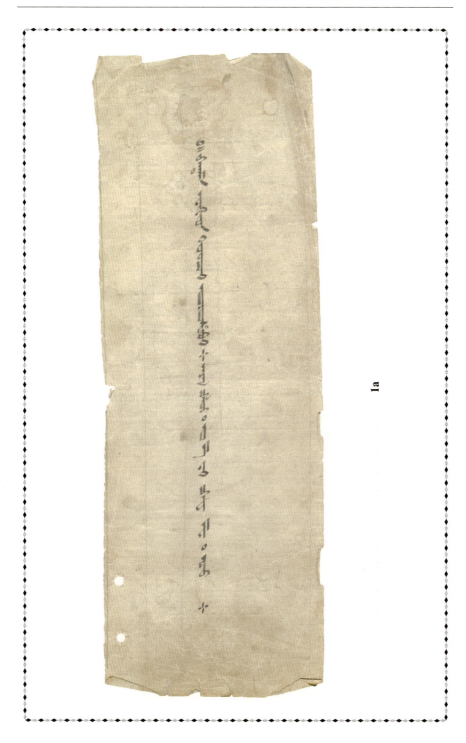

1a

1b

2a

2b

3a

3b

4a

4b

5a

5b

6a

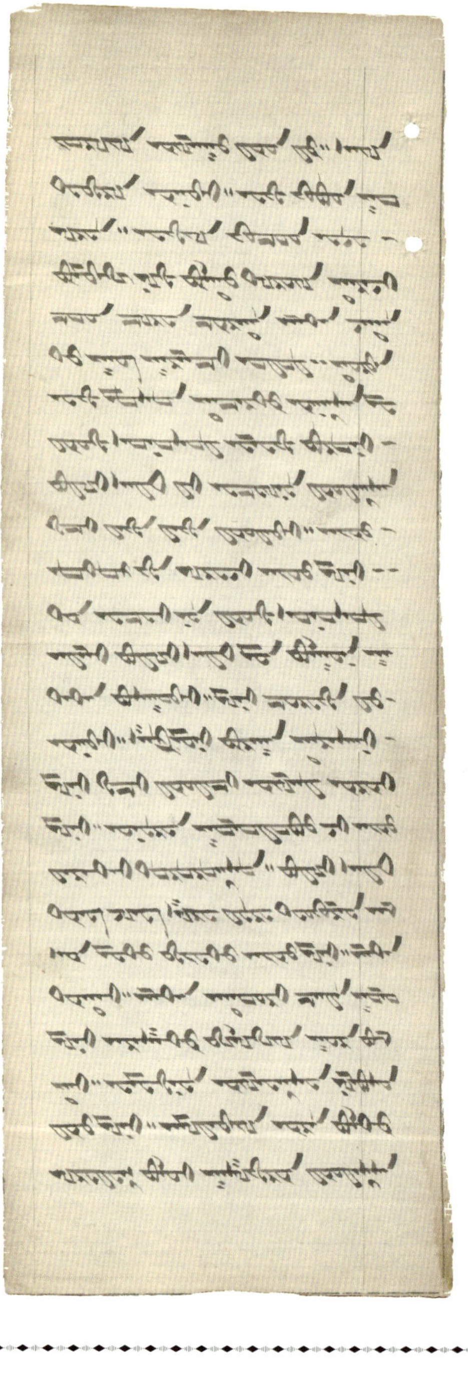

6b

7a

7b

8a

8b

9a

9b

10a

10b

11a

11b

12a

12b

13a

13b

14a

14b

15a

15b

16a

16b

17a

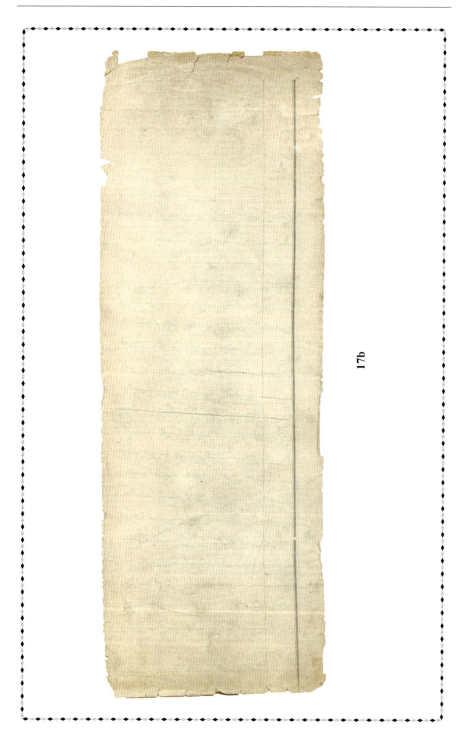

17b

罗斯勒·巴达木策仁所藏
《金刚手传规大黑天悉地经》

　　罗斯勒·巴达木策仁（1969—　　）新疆维吾尔自治区伊犁哈萨克自治州昭苏县羊场额鲁特人，牧民。属昭苏六苏木中的拿苏木人，乌兰库珠呼彤之额力根，抄经、诵经者——哈拉巴嘎希。

　　《金刚手传规大黑天悉地经》（《*sideti un toqtoɣal orošiboi*》）　成书年代不详，佚名。文献严重破损，多数看不清文字，清代金文抄本，7×15cm，3叶（双面）。

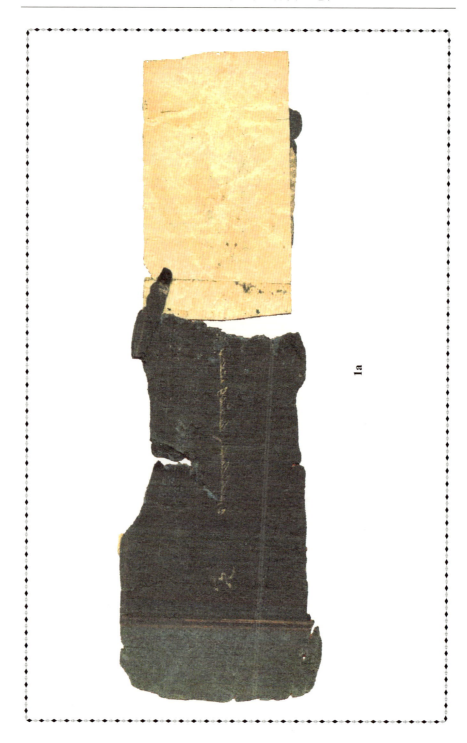

1a

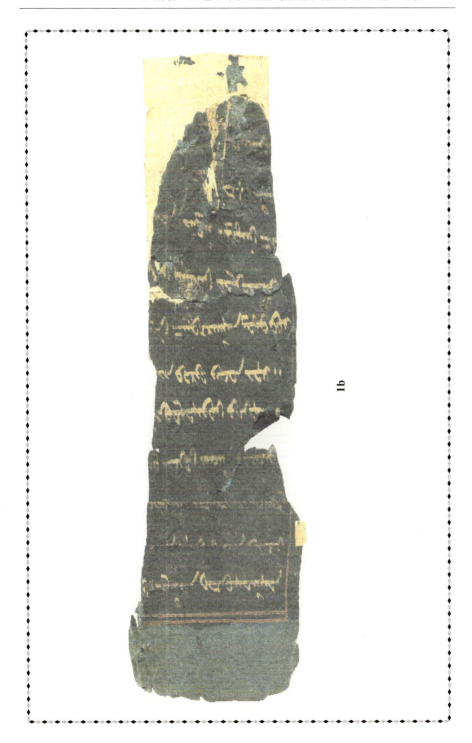

1b

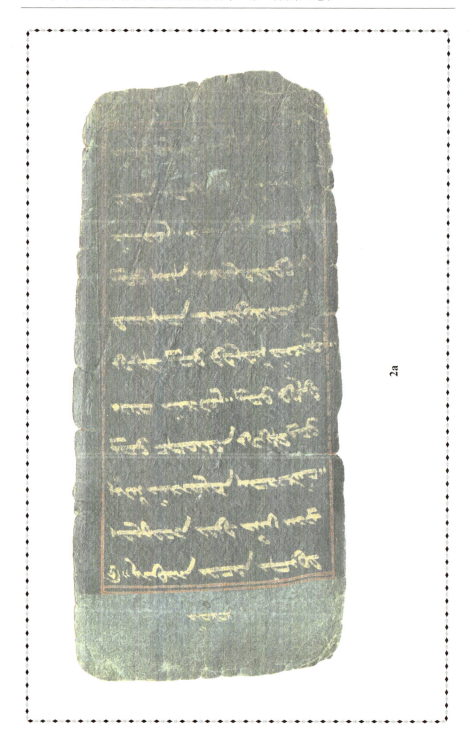

2a

2b

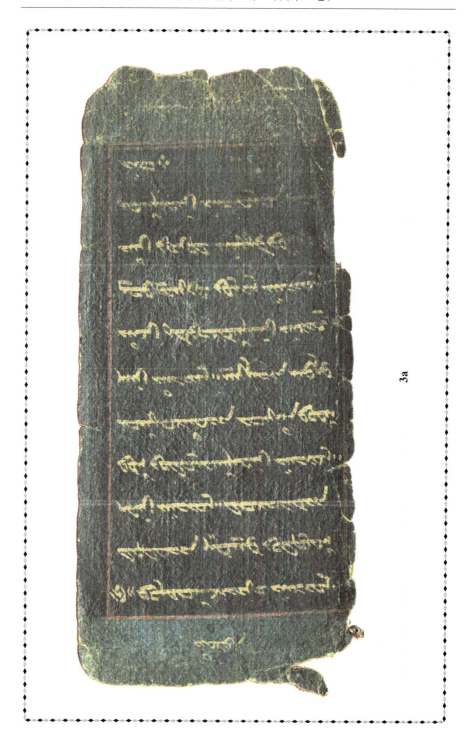

3a

3b

图书在版编目（CIP）数据

伊犁河流域额鲁特人托忒文文献荟萃. 第一辑：全三卷：蒙古语/
叶尔达主编 . —北京：中国社会科学出版社，2016.10
（大国学研究文库）
ISBN 978 – 7 – 5161 – 8496 – 7

Ⅰ.①伊…　Ⅱ.①叶…　Ⅲ.①厄鲁特—古籍—汇编—中国—蒙古语
（中国少数民族语言）　Ⅳ.①K289

中国版本图书馆 CIP 数据核字（2016）第 156686 号

出 版 人　赵剑英
责任编辑　史慕鸿
责任校对　李四新
责任印制　戴　宽

出　　版　中国社会科学出版社
社　　址　北京鼓楼西大街甲 158 号
邮　　编　100720
网　　址　http://www.csspw.cn
发 行 部　010 – 84083685
门 市 部　010 – 84029450
经　　销　新华书店及其他书店

印刷装订　北京君升印刷有限公司
版　　次　2016 年 10 月第 1 版
印　　次　2016 年 10 月第 1 次印刷

开　　本　710×1000　1/16
印　　张　58.25
字　　数　508 千字
定　　价　298.00 元（全三卷）

第三卷目录

第三卷

仁钦·尼帕所藏
《四部医典后续》

　　仁钦·尼帕（1974—　　）　　新疆维吾尔自治区伊犁哈萨克自治州昭苏县阿克达拉乡额鲁特人，农民。属昭苏六苏木中的阿合苏木人，门德额力根，诵经者——哈拉巴嘎希。

　　《四部医典后续》（《arašāni jüreken nayiman üyetü niɣuča obidšs xoyitu ündüsün kemekü orošiboi》）　　被誉为藏医药百科全书的《四部医典》之一，《四部医典》又称《医方四续》，公元8世纪著名藏医学家宇妥·宁玛云丹贡布所著。《四部医典后续》是《四部医典》中的一卷。17世纪卫拉特高僧咱雅班第达在和硕特部阿布赉台吉之倡议下翻译。清代抄本，10.5×48cm，92叶（双面），文献的开头以及结尾部分破损严重，目前唯独在伊犁河流域发现一部。

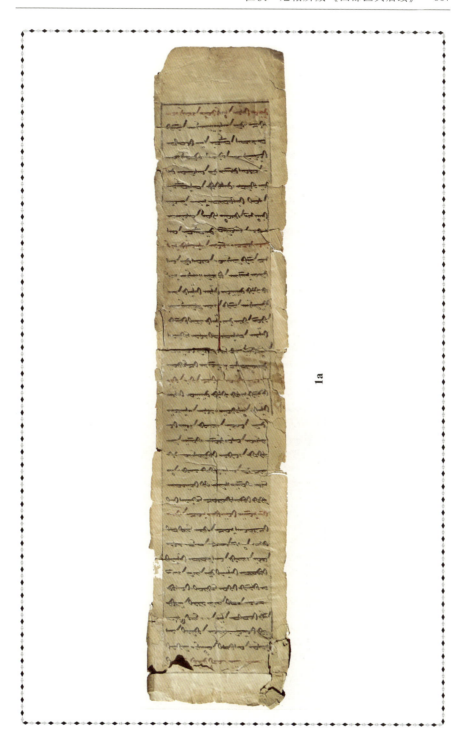

1a

2a

2b

3a

3b

4a

4b

5a

5b

6a

66b

7a

7b

8a

8b

9a

9b

10a

10b

11a

11b

12a

12b

13a

13b

14a

14b

15a

15b

16a

16b

17a

17b

18a

18b

19a

19b

20a

20b

21a

21b

22a

22b

23a

23b

24a

24b

25a

25b

26a

26b

27a

27b

28a

28b

29a

29b

30a

30b

31a

31b

32a

32b

33a

33b

34a

34b

35a

35b

36a

36b

37a

37b

38a

38b

39a

39b

40a

40b

41a

41b

42a

42b

43a

43b

44a

44b

45a

45b

46a

46b

47a

47b

48a

48b

49a

49b

50a

50b

51a

51b

52a

52b

53a

53b

54a

54b

55a

55b

56a

56b

57a

57b

58a

58b

59a

59b

60a

60b

61a

61b

62a

62b

63a

63b

64a

64b

65a

65b

66a

66b

67a

67b

68a

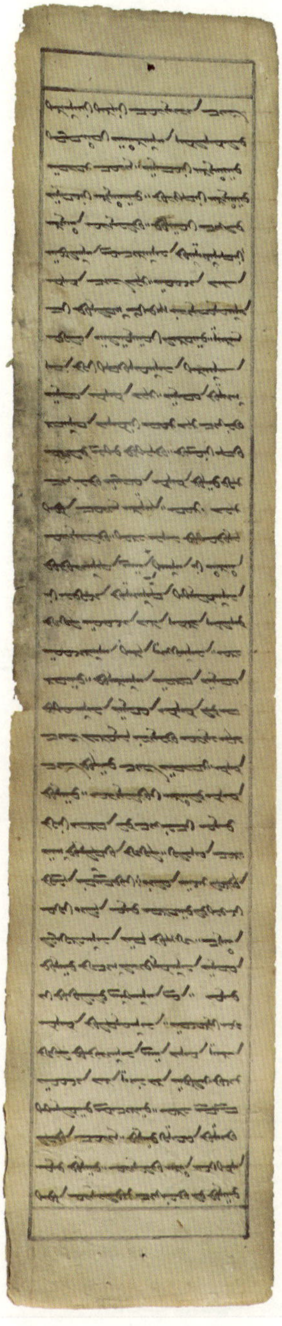

68b

69a

69b

70a

70b

71a

71b

72a

72b

73a

73b

74a

74b

75a

75b

76a

76b

77a

77b

78a

78b

79a

79b

80a

80b

81a

81b

82a

82b

83a

83b

84a

84b

85a

85b

86a

86b

87a

87b

88a

88b

89a

89b

90a

90b

91a

91b

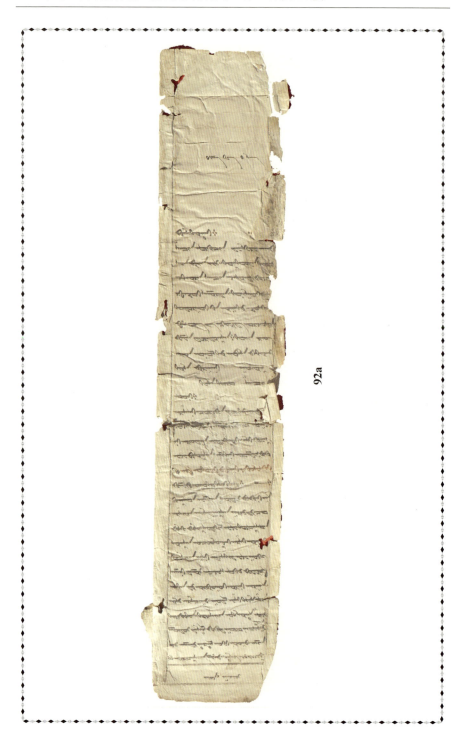

92a

92b

巴图图布欣·宾巴所藏
《宗喀巴大师传》

　　巴图图布欣·宾巴（1971—　）　　新疆维吾尔自治区伊犁哈萨克自治州昭苏县昭苏镇额鲁特人，个体户。属昭苏六苏木中的拿苏木人，奥日斯额力根，诵经者——哈拉巴嘎希。

　　《宗喀巴大师传》（《xoyoduγār yilaγuqsan nomyin xān boqdo zongkapa yin tuuǰi orošiboi》）　　托忒文重要传记，孤本。成书年代不详。清代抄本，10.5×30.5cm，47叶（双面），是黄教创始人宗喀巴大师传记。

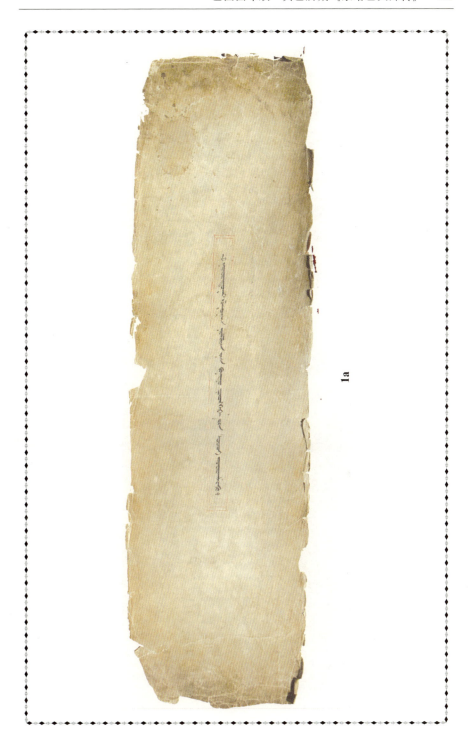

1a

1b

3a

3b

4a

4b

5a

5b

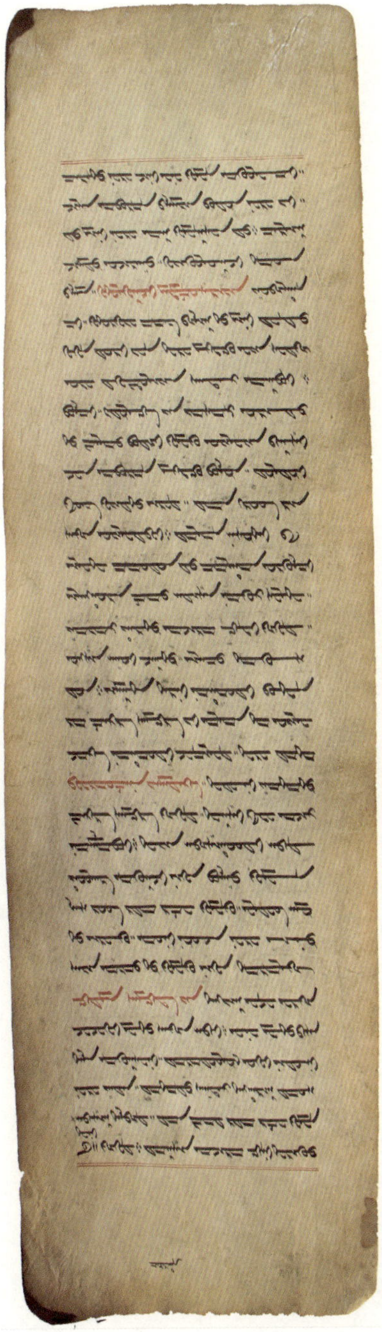

6a

7a

7b

8a

9a

9b

10a

10b

11a

11b

12a

12b

13a

13b

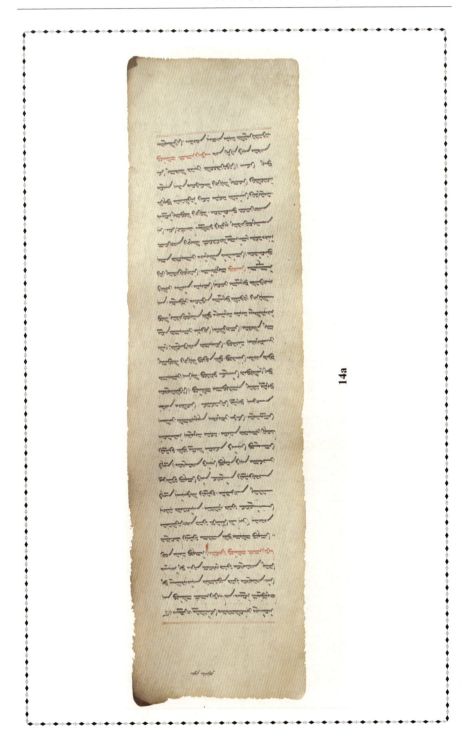

14a

14b

15a

15b

16a

16b

17a

17b

18a

18b

19a

19b

20a

20b

21a

21b

22a

22b

23a

23b

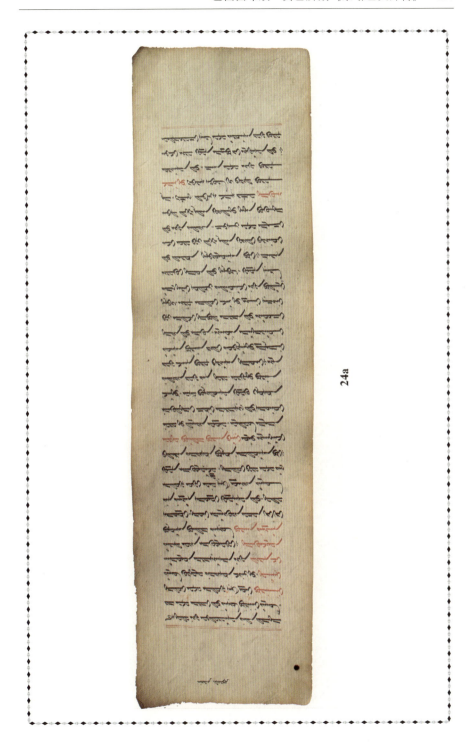

24a

25a

25b

26a

26b

27a

27b

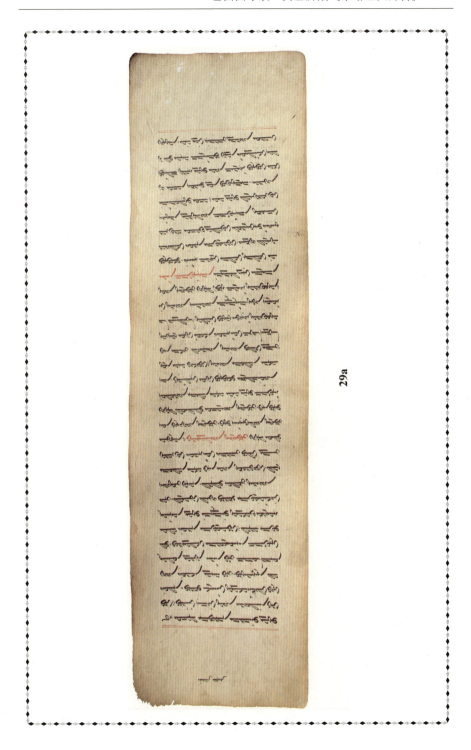

29a

29b

30a

30b

31a

31b

32a

32b

33a

33b

34a

34b

35a

35b

36a

36b

37a

37b

38a

38b

39a

39b

40a

40b

41a

41b

42a

42b

43a

43b

44a

44b

45a

45b

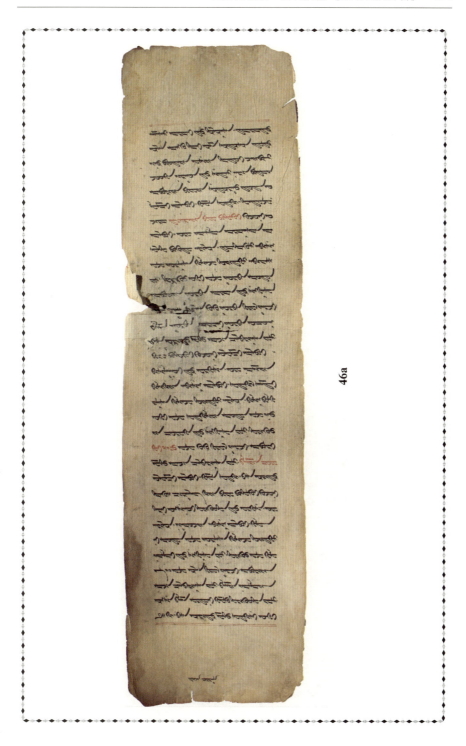

46a

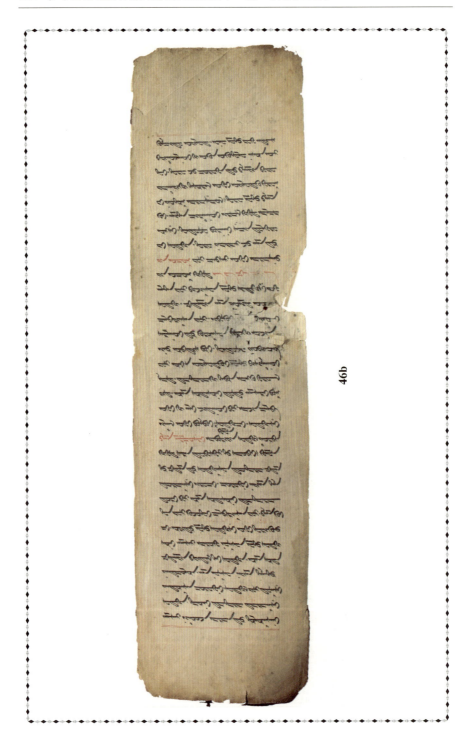

46b

47a

47b

希日盖·额布勒晋所藏
《五守护神大乘经集略》

　　希日盖·额布勒晋（1963—　　）　　新疆维吾尔自治区伊犁哈萨克自治州特克斯县土尔扈特人，牧民。属特克斯四苏木夏比纳尔中的英格苏木人，库勒策恩和之额力根，诵经者——哈拉巴嘎希。

　　《五守护神大乘经集略》（《banzaraqča yin xurngɣui orošiboi》）　　译经年代、译者不详，文献题目模糊不清，清代金文抄本，7.5×16cm，5叶（双面）。托忒文金文抄本甚少，该古籍尤为珍贵。

1a

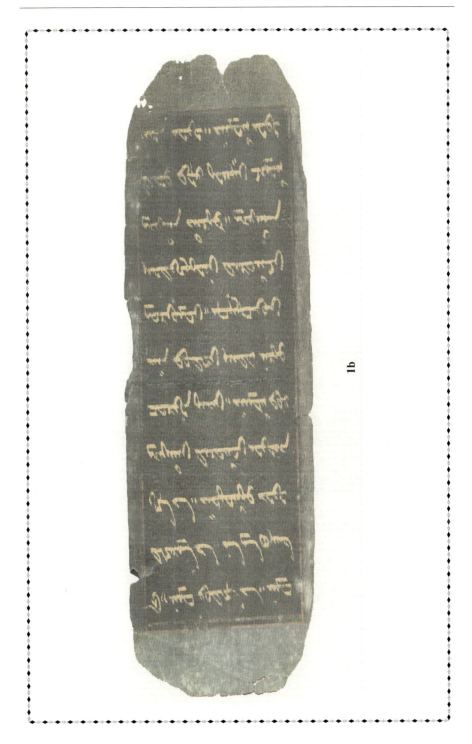

1b

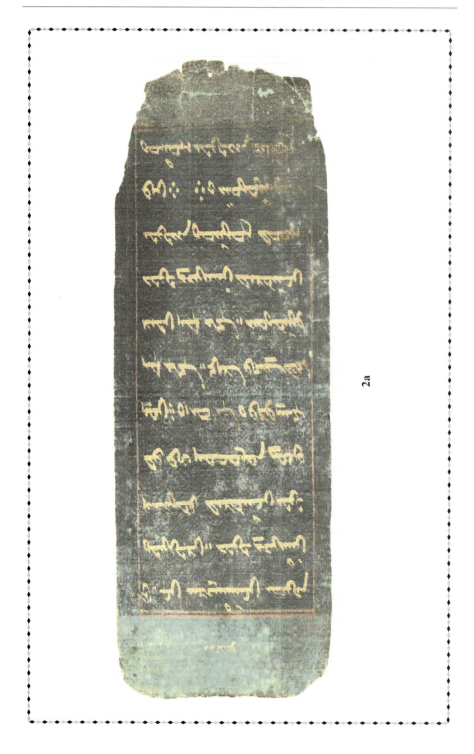

2a

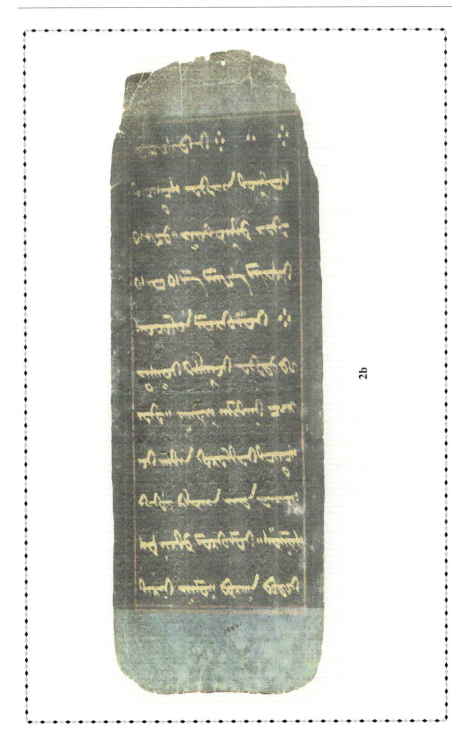

2b

3a

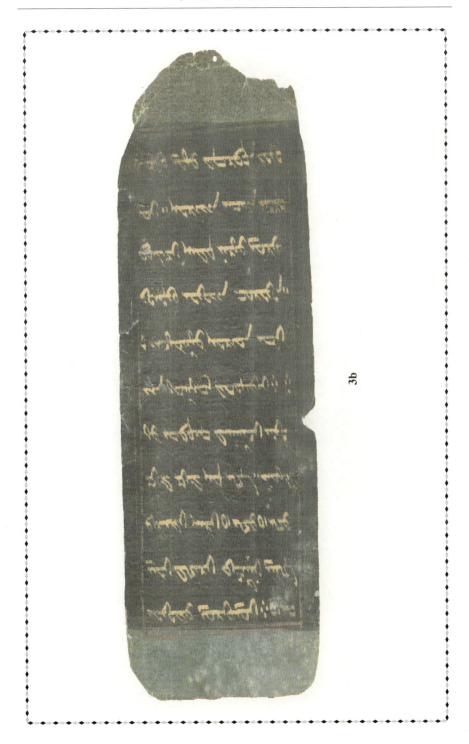

3b

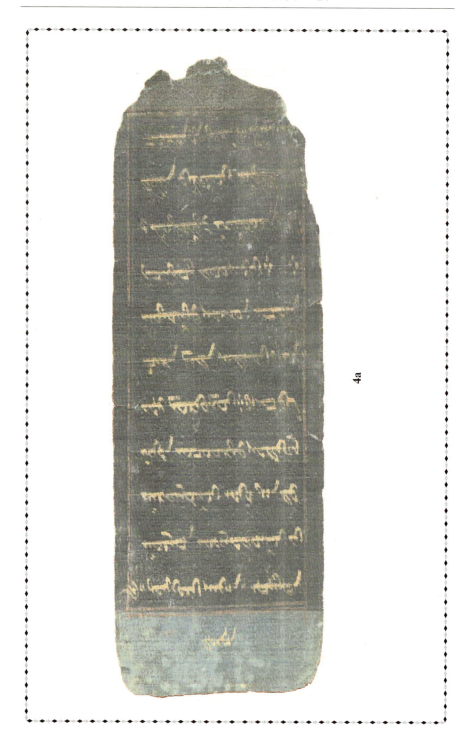

4a

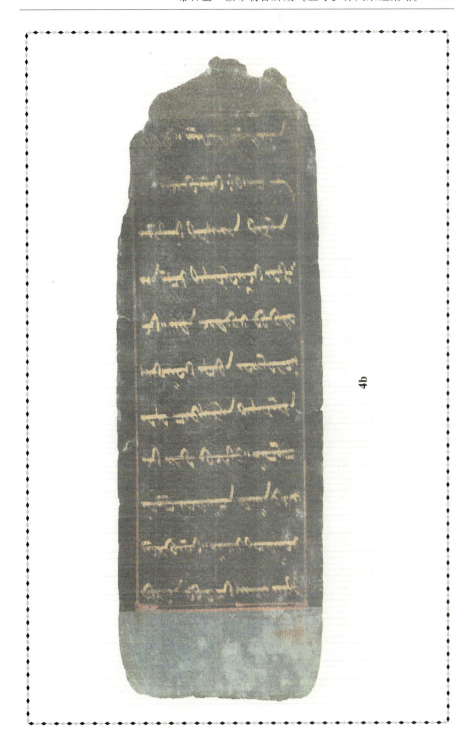

4b

5a

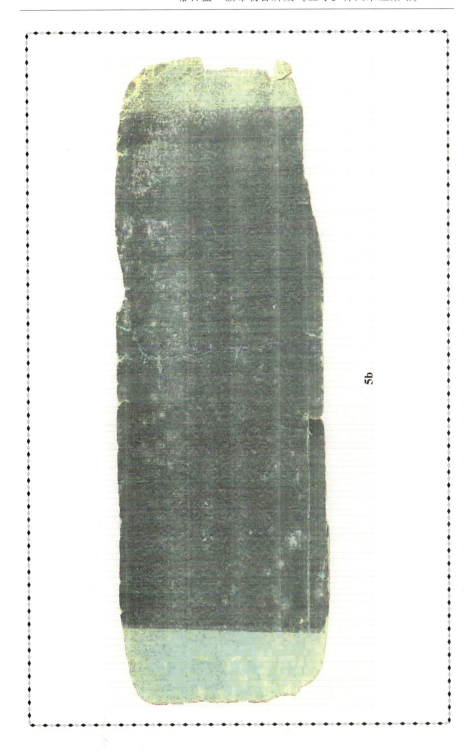

5b